Back To The Facts
Part 2

James Mitchell

Published by Robby Thiele & Rick Hofmann, Frankfurt, Germany

Book design by Robby Thiele

INTRODUCTION

At least since Donald Trump became president of the United States the term "Fake News" has become a synonym for everything that's wrong in our society. People cannot trust each other anymore and people specifically do not trust newspapers anymore. In a world where people start to trust strangers in shaky YouTube videos more than ever, we thought we must stop this development. We therefore roamed the continents and dug deep into many different subject areas on our search to uncover the real truth. The outcome is this book which tells you the facts that matter and that are far away from being fake news.

We hope this will give you a plenty of joy and more than a few surprises. Enjoy the read!

BACK TO THE FACTS – PART 2

Fact 1: If you could fold a piece of paper 42 times, that piece of paper would be able to reach the Moon.

Fact 2: Brryan Jackson's father infected his son with HIV at the age of eleven months to kill him, because he didn't want to pay alimony. Within 5 years the doctors diagnosed AIDS in Jackson. They gave him just a few months. Today, Brryan Jackson is 20 years old and HIV has not been detected in his blood for more than five years.

Fact 3: The Zoological Garden in Berlin is the largest zoo in the world.

Fact 4: So far about 270 people have had their bodies frozen, to be revived in the future.

Fact 5: In 2010 a pizza was sold for 10,000 Bitcoins. At today's exchange rate this would be four million dollars.

Fact 6: During the expansion of the railway network in Uganda, an incredible incident occurred. Two Tsavo lions repeatedly killed workers during night and slowed the construction progress. About 135 people died this way.

Fact 7: In 2006, scientists officially declared that the egg came first, not the chicken.

Fact 8: Studies show that people who live by the sea have lower levels of stress than others. Scientists suspect that the color blue may have a strong influence on stress levels.

Fact 9: After Billy Owen lost part of his face and his right eye to cancer, he began a career as a zombie actor for numerous movies and series.

Fact 10: During the Second World War, British soldier Digby Tatham-Warter was known among his comrades for always taking an umbrella along into battle so that his own comrades could identify him better and would not accidentally shoot him. He even managed to capture a German car after stabbing the driver in the eye with his umbrella.

Fact 11: There are more public libraries in the U.S. than McDonald's restaurants.

Fact 12: Because intelligent people think faster, their handwriting is sloppier.

Fact 13: By law, cars are prohibited on Mackinac Island in Michigan since 1898. Inhabitants use horses instead.

Fact 14: It has been established that whenever actress Anne Hathaway is trending in social media, automated investment bank trading algorithms automatically buy more shares in Berkshire Hathaway.

Fact 15: Playing video games increases creativity, concentration and makes you happier.

Fact 16: Algerian hacker Hamza Bendelladj stole 280 million dollars from over 200 banks and donated most of the money to aid organizations in Palestine. In 2015, he was sentenced to 30 years in prison in the United States.

Fact 17: The average rent for a one room apartment in Manhattan is 3,400 dollars.

Fact 18: Based on the number of units sold, "Candle in the Wind" by Elton John is the most successful single of all times. All in all, more than 37 million CDs were sold worldwide.

Fact 19: Adult cats exclusively meow to communicate with humans.

Fact 20: If 57 people are gathered in one room, the likelihood of two of the people having their birthday on the same day, is about 99 percent.

Fact 21: Kit Kat is very popular in Japan. The Japanese expression "Kitto Katsu" loosely translates as "safe profit", which has led to Japanese people often giving away a Kit Kat to wish someone luck.

Fact 22: According to a survey conducted in 2000, Japanese people think that instant noodles are the greatest Japanese invention of the 20th century.

Fact 23: The first American woman to receive a doctorate in computer science was a nun.

Fact 24: Currently, there are about seven billion people on earth who make experiences and memories every day. A total of 220 years of new human memories are generated per second.

Fact 25: The average fee to cross the Panama Canal by ship is 54,000 dollars.

Fact 26: Barry Marshall was firmly convinced that not stress but rather Helicobacter pylori bacteria are the main cause of stomach ulcers. In a self-experiment in 1984, he therefore drank a test tube of the bacteria and shortly thereafter developed severe gastritis, which he successfully cured with antibiotics. In 2005, he was awarded the Nobel Prize for his research on Helicobacter pylori together with John Robin Warren.

Fact 27: Google Street View also allows you to view images of remote locations such as the Great Barrier Reef in Australia.

Fact 28: On average, German women have their first baby at the age of 29.

Fact 29: In Japan, it is socially acceptable to sleep while working. It is perceived as a sign of hard work.

Fact 30: The most common fracture in the human body is the collarbone.

Fact 31: The human circadian rhythm is better suited to life on Mars than on Earth.

Fact 32: Netflix has over 20 million subscribers in China, even though Netflix is not available in China at all.

Fact 33: Frequently asked questions at a Microsoft job interview are: "Why are manhole covers round?" and "Design a coffee machine that can be used by astronauts".

Fact 34: Three men from Yemen accused NASA for "settling" on Mars. According to the men, their ancestors gave it to them 3,000 years ago.

Fact 35: In the last 3,000 years, there were only 268 years in which no wars occurred.

Fact 36: The Tammar wallaby has a weight of only one gram at birth.

Fact 37: At a wedding ceremony, women usually stand to the left of the groom. This has historical reasons, as this way the man's sword hand was free to protect the woman from any attackers.

Fact 38: In 2013, a plane crash-landed in San Francisco, killing two girls. As it turned out, one of them died not as a result of the crash, but because of a careless ambulance driver.

Fact 39: Due to global warming, the sea level rises approximately three millimeters each year.

Fact 40: The shortest commercial flight lasts only 47 seconds and brings people in Scotland from the Westray Island to Papa Westray Island.

Fact 41: In the last 150 years, the average body size of a human has increased by four inches.

Fact 42: The two great Cuban revolutionaries - Che Guevara and Fidel Castro - both have a doctorate degree. Che was a medical doctor, Fidel a lawyer.

Fact 43: It is estimated that there are more than 270 million fake accounts on Facebook.

Fact 44: In the British Army only soldiers ranked "Pioneer Sergeant" are allowed to have a beard.

Fact 45: Dinosaurs lived on earth for 170 million years. In contrast, humans (Homo Sapiens) have only been around for 300,000 years.

Fact 46: In 2012, the author of the book series "Fifty Shades of Grey" - E. L. James - was the most successful author of the year.

Fact 47: Polar bears are left-handed.

Fact 48: The International Space Station is the most expensive object ever made by humans. It has cost 160 billion dollars so far.

Fact 49: During World War II, the U.S. Army collaborated with Walt Disney to develop a gas mask that looked like Mickey Mouse, in order to make children less afraid of a poison gas attack.

Fact 50: In ancient Rome, black people were considered absolutely equal in society.

Fact 51: In the 1960s, a female fan hid in postal package and was sent by a friend to the Beatles' address. The postal services however, discovered and freed the lady before she was able to be posted.

Fact 52: Burger King offers free burgers for life to celebrities who want to promote their fast food.

Fact 53: An estimated 11 quadrillion tons of diamonds are hidden at a depth of 90 to 150 miles under the earth's surface.

Fact 54: It has been scientifically proven that petting a dog can significantly reduce blood pressure in humans.

Fact 55: The largest playable violin in the world weighs 289 pounds.

Fact 56: Over an investigation period from 1985 to 2012, scientists were able to show that Greenland is the country with the highest suicide rate. During this period, 83 out of 100,000 people committed suicide, while 20 percent of the population reported to have attempted suicide at least once before.

Fact 57: In 2013, scientists added human brain cells to a mouse, and it actually went on to demonstrate improved cognitive abilities.

Fact 58: The largest hydrogen bomb that has been detonated caused such a big shock wave that it could still be measured after the third circumnavigation of the globe.

Fact 59: Before English became the dominant language in the U.S., German was the second most common language.

Fact 60: The "Jesus nut" is the bolt that holds the rotor blades of a helicopter together. The name of the bolt was given by its importance. When it breaks, only a prayer to Jesus helps one to survive.

Fact 61: Big Major Cay is an island in the Bahamas that is almost exclusively populated by pigs. To this day, it has not been clearly ascertained how the pigs got to the island.

Fact 62: It was not until 2013 that the US government officially confirmed the existence of its "Area 51" test site.

Fact 63: There is 4G reception on Mount Everest.

Fact 64: In 2000, Iraqi dictator Saddam Hussein, published the novel "Zabibah and the King", which tells the story of a ruler in ancient Babylon and a simple girl who fall in love. The book sold over a million copies in Iraq and became a bestseller. It was even adapted for a TV series and a musical.

Fact 65: Before Netflix streamed films, customers could have DVDs sent to them by mail. Due to the volume of customers and the large number of films and series, Netflix at times became the largest customer of the US Postal Service.

Fact 66: The Italian chocolate brand "Italo Suisse" changed its name in 2013 to "Isis". One year later it had to change it again because of the rise of the terror organization.

Fact 67: To protect the German soldiers from the British night vision technology, they spread the lie that eating lots of carrots helped British soldiers to increase their eyesight during night. A myth was born.

Fact 68: When Queen Elizabeth visited the set of "Game of Thrones", she was asked if she would like to sit on the Iron Throne. However, she declined, as she is not allowed to sit on a foreign throne.

Fact 69: After John Pemberton was wounded in the American Civil War, he became addicted to morphine. In order to free himself from the drug, he developed his own painkiller, which he made from cocaine and alcohol. In 1886 he designed a non-alcoholic variant that was later sold under the name "Coca-Cola".

Fact 70: In Germany, prisoners who are to be released in January can apply for a Christmas amnesty. If the request is granted, the prisoner is allowed to leave the prison earlier in order to spend Christmas with his family.

Fact 71: Throughout the story of "How I Met Your Mother," there were only twelve incidents in which Barney Stinson did not wear a suit.

Fact 72: In medieval France, women were among others punished by being forced to catch a chicken in the city while naked.

Fact 73: Human blood contains about 0.2 milligrams of gold.

Fact 74: Some national flags contain another small flag. This "flag in a flag" is called a "jack" and is always placed in the upper left corner, as this is the most visible area of a flag.

Fact 75: "Hikikomori" is the term used in Japan to describe people who withdraw completely from social life and do not wish to have contact with other people.

Fact 76: The fast food chain Subway has over 41,000 restaurants. This means that on average, two restaurants have been opened per day since its establishment in 1965.

Fact 77: If you bathe in alcohol, you can get drunk.

Fact 78: Red-haired people produce more vitamin D than people with a different hair color.

Fact 79: About 99 percent of all Estonians have blue eyes.

Fact 80: When physicist Niels Bohr won the Nobel Prize, the Carlsberg Brewery gave him a house right next to the brewery with a beer pipe leading directly from the brewery into the house. Until the end of his life, Niels Bohr could drink as much beer as he wanted free of charge.

Fact 81: The most common first name in Italy is Russo.

Fact 82: British woman Wendy Southgate is most commonly seen on Google Street View.

Fact 83: For safety reasons, the Guinness Book of World Records does not accept record attempts on how long a person can stay awake. The last registered record dates back to 1964 and is eleven days and 25 minutes.

Fact 84: When crying tears of joy, the first one mainly comes from the right eye, while the first tear of sorrow mostly comes from the left.

Fact 85: A study proved that men really have problems understanding women's feelings.

Fact 86: When Saudi King Salman travels in his private jet, he always takes a golden escalator along to exit the plane.

Fact 87: Donald Duck's second name is "Fauntleroy".

Fact 88: Ten percent of all Germans don't know why they celebrate Christmas.

Fact 89: The guitarist of the rock band Queen has a doctorate in astrophysics.

Fact 90: During the production of "Toy Story 2", an employee accidentally erased the whole movie and almost ruined the production. Fortunately, one of the employees had a backup on her desktop computer, so the work went on and the movie made it to the cinemas.

Fact 91: Dutchman Wim Hof can withstand even extremely cold temperatures, earning him the nickname "The Iceman". He climbed Mount Everest up to a height of 21.982 feet wearing only shorts and shoes, ran a marathon in the Arctic at -4 degrees Fahrenheit wearing nothing but shorts and holds the world record for the longest time a person has endured in a block of ice: one hour 52 minutes and 42 seconds.

Fact 92: In the USA, more money is spent on slot machines than on cinema, baseball and amusement parks combined.

Fact 93: As Burger King has no rights to its brand name in Australia, the fast food chain is called "Hungry Jack's" there.

Fact 94: A "moment" is a medieval time unit, exactly 90 seconds. An hour therefore has 40 moments.

Fact 95: The more strenuous a mental task is, the larger a person's pupils become.

Fact 96: The female form of the Indian-Hindu ruler's title "Maharajah" is "Maharani".

Fact 97: Cymothoa exigua, a parasitic isopod, is the only known parasite that can replace an entire body part of its host. First, the parasite feeds on the tongue of a fish until it completely replaces it and in doing so takes over the tongue's function.

Fact 98: About 83 percent of German women would abstain from sex for 100,000 Euros.

Fact 99: Male reindeer shed their antlers every year at Christmas time. However, since Santa's reindeer all have antlers, they must be either female or neutered.

Fact 100: About every eight days, sloths climb down to the ground to have a bowel movement.

Fact 101: The human is the only primate who has no bone in his penis.

Fact 102: In war times significantly more boys than girls are born. This is called the "Returning Soldier Syndrome".

Fact 103: When Wilhelm Röntgen discovered a new form of radiation, he could not think of a suitable name for this phenomenon, so he simply called it X-radiation. This is the reason why to this day the rays are called "X rays" in English, while in German-speaking countries they are known as "Röntgen rays".

Fact 104: Everyday McDonald's serves over 68 million people. This is approximately one percent of the world's population.

Fact 105: The sport of badminton was initially called "Poona".

Fact 106: Pac-Man was originally named "Puck Man"

Fact 107: By his 13th birthday, Mike Tyson had already been arrested 38 times.

Fact 108: The first Google Doodle was the Google logo including a Burning Man stick figure and came out on the 30th of August 1998. The intention for it was to show everybody that both founders Page and Brin attended the festival.

Fact 109: From 1789 to 1790, New York was the capital of the USA.

Fact 110: In the Arabic versions of the cult show, Homer Simpson drinks water instead of beer.

Fact 111: There are just two people who know the recipe for Coca Cola. For this reason they are not allowed to be in a plane at the same time.

Fact 112: The superhero Flash is faster than Superman.

Fact 113: There is a large dark spot at the North Pole of Pluto's moon Charon, and scientists have no idea what it is. They therefore called it Mordor, in reference to the mysterious dark land in "The Lord of the Rings".

Fact 114: For a long time, it was tradition in Ireland that one liter of Guinness beer was given for each liter of donated blood.

Fact 115: 27-year-old American Cassandra De Pecol is the first woman to travel to all the sovereign nations of the world. She managed to reach the 196 countries in less than 19 months and with that also holds the world record for visiting all countries of the world in the shortest amount of time.

Fact 116: Greyhounds can reach speeds of more than 68 miles per hour and are therefore almost as fast as cheetahs.

Fact 117: Before McDonald's offered burgers, the company sold hot dogs.

Fact 118: Corals are chemically so similar to human bones that they are used to treat fractures.

Fact 119: The scientific name for the western lowland gorilla is "Gorilla gorilla gorilla".

Fact 120: Alaska crosses the border with the eastern hemisphere and is thus the most eastern and western state in the USA.

Fact 121: Bob Marley's song "No Woman No Cry" was actually called "No Woman Nuh Cry". This song is not about the better life of men without women, but about the life of a sad woman.

Fact 122: During the making of the film "Star Wars - Return of the Jedi Knights" a number of crew members surrounded the actor playing Chewbacca in forest scenes to guarantee his safety. They were afraid that hunters might think he was Bigfoot.

Fact 123: Karl Marx named all four of his daughters Jenny after his wife Jenny Marx.

Fact 124: The inner skin of a vagina is folded and opens while having sex.

Fact 125: Walter Summerford was struck by lightning in his life three times. After he died, his gravestone was also struck by lightning.

Fact 126: The temperature scales Fahrenheit and Celsius meet at -40 degrees. So therefore -40° F = -40° C.

Fact 127: Even during the night there are rainbows. They are called "moon bows".

Fact 128: Mark Zuckerberg, the founder of Facebook, receives a fixed annual salary of just one dollar.

Fact 129: At the US Arlington National Cemetery, there is a group of women who call themselves the "Arlington Ladies". Since their inception in 1948, they have voluntarily committed themselves to attend every funeral ceremony in Arlington so that no soldier needs to be buried alone. On average, the women attend 30 funerals a week.

Fact 130: In 1906, the physicist J. J. Thompson won the Nobel Prize for his proof that electrons are particles. 31 years later his son also received the Nobel Prize for his proof that electrons are a wave.

Fact 131: In order to protect Tokyo from being flooded by typhoons, a gigantic underground system of tunnels and water pumps was developed underneath the city. It can pump 220 tons of water into the underground per second.

Fact 132: Nutella was invented during World War II, when an Italian soldier mixed chocolate with hazelnut to stretch his food ration.

Fact 133: Astronauts in the ISS can witness 15 sunrises and 15 sunsets a day.

Fact 134: Hyperlinks were already blue in the early days of the Internet.

Fact 135: The first person to give weather phenomena human names was the American Clement Wragge. He decided to name hurricanes after politicians in order to allow witty allusions to their political activities. The system has remained in place to this day.

Fact 136: Google considers more than 200 factors for the calculation of its search results.

Fact 137: To find out whether a female is capable of mating, male giraffes beat their heads on the female's belly until they urinate. The male can determine the female's fertility by the smell of her urine.

Fact 138: In 2016, at the age of 104, Jack Reynolds from Great Britain became the oldest person to get a tattoo. One year later, he became the oldest person to ride a roller coaster.

Fact 139: Diabetic patients are unable to regulate their blood glucose level. For this reason, the glucose level is sometimes so high that even the urine of a diabetic patient would taste sweet.

Fact 140: James Harrison is a record holder in blood donations. He donated his blood over 1,000 times.

Fact 141: McDonald's sells 75 burgers per minute.

Fact 142: Bhutan is the only country in the world with a negative CO_2 balance. The country's constitution stipulates that at least 60 percent of the land mass must be covered with forest.

Fact 143: Stephen Hawking's tombstone bears the formula he developed to calculate the entropy of black holes. He had requested this long before his death. Hawking was also buried near the graves of Isaac Newton and Charles Darwin.

Fact 144: At a height of almost 12 miles and above the air pressure is so low, that water in your body would vaporize due your own body temperature.

Fact 145: There are so many languages in the world that it is not known how many there currently are. Scientists believe that there are more than 6,500 to 7,000 different languages.

Fact 146: The dress that Princess Diana wore on her wedding with Prince Charles had a 26 feet long train.

Fact 147: The former U.S. Marine soldier Guy Gabaldon was able to catch about 800 Japanese soldiers during World War Two. The Japanese soldiers were hiding in a cave and Guy Gabaldon sneaked in. He convinced them that their cave was surrounded. After everyone was handcuffed he called for support.

Fact 148: Robert Downey Jr. was the only actor who was allowed to read the entire script of "Avengers: Endgame".

Fact 149: Originally, Mickey Mouse was called Mortimer Mouse.

Fact 150: When the Millennium Bridge in London was completed in the year 2000, pedestrians almost caused it to collapse. Due to a slight natural oscillation of the bridge, the people crossed it in lockstep so that a resonance occurred. The bridge started swinging so strongly that it had to be closed only two days after its opening in order to make appropriate improvements.

Fact 151: After being hit by an avalanche, the arctic scientist Peter Freuchen freed himself by making a chisel from his frozen stool. After this, he amputated his frostbitten toes with a hammer.

Fact 152: In the early 1980s, Pablo Escobar was responsible for 80 percent of the world's cocaine production.

Fact 153: If a stalactite combines with a stalagmite to form a large pillar, this is called a stalagnate.

Fact 154: One of the original ingredients of Coca-Cola was cocaine

Fact 155: In 2001, a study concluded that murder was the most common cause of death among pregnant women in the United States between 1993 and 1998.

Fact 156: Rhnull (rhesus factor zero) is the rarest blood type in the world. So far, only 40 people worldwide are known to have this blood group.

Fact 157: Kizhi Pogost is a church in Russia which was built more than 300 years ago and is made exclusively from wood. It is over 115 feet high and does not contain a single nail.

Fact 158: The word "Tsundoku" is Japanese and describes people who buy many books but never read them.

Fact 159: With a height of 8.23 inches, Sultan Kösen from Turkey is the tallest man in the world. He has shoe size 62 and the distance from his wrist to the tip of his middle finger is 11.2 inches.

Fact 160: A "kakistocracy" is a system of government where a country is ruled by the worst and least qualified persons.

Fact 161: During World War II, women in France who had relations with German soldiers were shaved bald so that everyone could see that they had betrayed their country.

Fact 162: In the 1940s, the Coca Cola Company developed a colorless version of Coca Cola specifically for the USSR.

Fact 163: The vampire bat has an enzyme that prevents its victims' blood from clotting on wounds. As a result, the victims lose more blood that the vampire bats can then feed on.

Fact 164: Ioannis Economou, the chief translator of the European Parliament, speaks 32 languages fluently.

Fact 165: Africa is the world's poorest continent. It accounts for just 2.4% of global Gross Domestic Product.

Fact 166: Russia has more land mass than Pluto.

Fact 167: "Point Nemo" is the place on the earth's surface that is furthest away from any mainland or island. It is located in the southern Pacific Ocean, 1,670 miles from the nearest mainland. Even the astronauts on the ISS space station are closer to this point than any other person on the mainland anywhere.

Fact 168: Because emus and kangaroos are not able to walk backwards, they are officially referred to as heraldic animals of Australia.

Fact 169: Termite mounds are built in such a way that the climate inside always remains approximately the same, even if major weather changes occur. Nevertheless, fresh air constantly enters the mound while pollutants are removed.

Fact 170: Dallol is an area in Northern Ethiopia and has the highest average temperature on Earth. The average temperature is 93 degrees Fahrenheit (34 degrees Celsius).

Fact 171: Twelve newborn babies are given to false parents every day.

Fact 172: The Vatican has released a church version of Pokémon Go. The game is called "Follow JC Go", and instead of Pokémon you "catch" saints.

Fact 173: When Playmobil was launched on the market in the 1970s, a construction worker set was available that included a small plastic beer crate.

Fact 174: The molecule Penguinone got its name because of its chemical structure which resembles a penguin.

Fact 175: During World War II, the French weightlifter Charles Rigoulet was sent to a Nazi prison. He broke out by bending the metal rods of his prison cell and was even able to free several other fellow prisoners.

Fact 176: As a student at Columbia University, Ken Hechtman stole uranium-238. He later broke into Area 51, became a reporter and after the events of 9/11 illegally entered Afghanistan, where he was ultimately taken hostage by the Taliban.

Fact 177: "Chauffeur" is the French word for heater, because the first cars were steam-powered and had to be heated.

Fact 178: Neptune, Saturn and Venus are the names of three seaside resorts in Romania.

Fact 179: Almost 90 percent of all alpacas worldwide live exclusively in Peru.

Fact 180: Cats have 32 muscles to move their ears. In comparison, humans only have six muscles in their ears.

Fact 181: Women suffering from "hyperlactation syndrome" produce excessive amounts of breast milk - up to 1.6 gallons of milk a day. A woman's average milk production is usually less than 0.3 gallons per day.

Fact 182: The longest beard ever measured on a woman had a length of 10 inches.

Fact 183: It is estimated that 7,000 people die every year because the handwriting of the treating doctor was not legible.

Fact 184: George Lucas obtained the rights to the word "droid". When Motorola released a cell phone with this name, they had to pay a fee to George Lucas.

Fact 185: The Scully effect is the term used to describe the fact that after the TV series "The X-Files" was broadcast, women became increasingly interested in scientific professions. The reason for this was the female protagonist Dana Scully, who solved curious cases for the FBI thanks to her medical studies.

Fact 186: Rabbits have such good peripheral sight they are able to see things behind their head.

Fact 187: According to FIFA, the five meter space of a football field must be 5.50 meters wide.

Fact 188: "Fox tossing" was a popular sport in the 16th century in which two people held a 23-foot-long cloth on both sides and then pulled it tight as soon as a fox ran over the cloth so that it flew into the air. The game continued until the animal broke its bones when it hit the ground and was then killed by a hunter.

Fact 189: 50,000 people die a year in the U.S. from the effects of passive smoking.

Fact 190: During World War II, Adolf Hitler gave the order to spare the British city of Blackpool from bomb attacks, as he intended to go on holiday there after Germany had won the war.

Fact 191: Sea otters hold hands when they sleep to avoid drifting apart from each other.

Fact 192: Television preacher Oral Roberts once told his viewers that God would kill him if he did not receive eight million dollars from them. In the end, the viewers even sent him more than nine million dollars.

Fact 193: The Pomato is a hybrid between a tomato and a potato. The plant produces both tomatoes and potatoes.

Fact 194: If classical music is played in wine shops, the turnover increases by 2.5 times compared to the wine shops where pop music is played.

Fact 195: In order to avoid a long-standing dispute, the CEO's of Southwest Airline and Stevens Aviation decided to resolve their problem by arm wrestling. The winner was given the right to use a specific advertising slogan.

Fact 196: Around the region of the Ecuadorian city of Quito, a large number of the inhabitants suffer from a special form of dwarfism. The genetic mutation which inhibits growth also protects those affected from all forms of cancer and diabetes.

Fact 197: Don Juan Pond in Antarctica is the saltiest body of water on earth. Its salt content is over 40 percent.

Fact 198: "Bart Gets an F" - the first episode of the second season of "The Simpsons", is the most watched Simpsons episode.

Fact 199: The website "godtube.com" describes itself as YouTube for Christians.

Fact 200: People who own iPhones have sex more often compared to Android users.

Fact 201: Termites eat their food at double the speed when heavy metal is played.

Fact 202: Each year, about one million new employees are hired by McDonald's in the U.S.

Fact 203: Africa is the hottest continent on earth.

Fact 204: The color that the human eye perceives in complete darkness is called "Eigengrau" (German for "intrinsic gray").

Fact 205: Annually, more people die from being hit by a champagne cork than from the bite of a venomous spider.

Fact 206: John Adams, the second president of the United States once said "I have come to the conclusion that one useless man is called a disgrace; that two are called a law firm; and that three or more become a Congress!"

Fact 207: Robert Lane named his two sons "Winner" and "Loser". Winner Lane turned criminal, while Loser Lane had a successful career at the NYPD.

Fact 208: In Australia, a hog stole 18 beers from a camping site, got drunk and then tried to attack a cow.

Fact 209: The Greenland shark does not reach sexual maturity until the age of 150. With an estimated life expectancy of up to 500 years, it is also the longest living vertebrate on the planet.

Fact 210: In France, the national fencing federation recognized light saber fencing as an official competitive sport in 2019. Instead of saber, foil or sword, the fighters use replicas of light sabers from Star Wars. With this campaign, the association hopes to get more young people interested in fencing.

Fact 211: It takes 40 minutes to cook an ostrich egg.

Fact 212: A fully-grown elephant can drink about 53 gallons of water within five minutes.

Fact 213: Babies can already get an erection in the womb.

Fact 214: As the water of a coconut is isotonic and sterile, it is used as saline solution in underdeveloped countries.

Fact 215: The largest cinema in the world is the Kinépolis in Madrid, with a total of 25 different screening rooms and 9,200 seats.

Fact 216: Until 1809, Finland was officially only a part of Sweden.

Fact 217: In Finland, there are more saunas than cars. There are a total of 2.2 million saunas for 5.4 million inhabitants.

Fact 218: The capital of Kazakhstan is Astana. Which when translated means "capital".

Fact 219: The first successful blood transfusion took place in 1660 and was between two dogs.

Fact 220: In the 20th century, there were still stomach-breeding frogs living in Australia. The tadpoles grew up in the mother's stomach and climbed out of her mouth as soon as they were big enough.

Fact 221: There is no city that is more often destroyed in movies than New York.

Fact 222: In the state prison of Indiana, the occupants may keep cats.

Fact 223: On 9 August 1965, Singapore was officially expelled from Malaysia, making it the first country to involuntarily gain independence.

Fact 224: In 1997, Microsoft employed 31,000 people worldwide, of which 21,000 already were millionaires because of their participation in the company.

Fact 225: To prepare for her tour, Beyoncé always sings while jogging.

Fact 226: The "Medical Students Disease" describes the phenomenon of medical students suffering from the disease they recently have learned about in class.

Fact 227: During his time in school Isaac Newton wrote an essay on how water moves from the roots to the leaves in a tree. This phenomenon could first be scientifically proven about 225 years later.

Fact 228: Mel Blanc, who became famous as the voice of Bugs Bunny, was allergic to carrots.

Fact 229: The human eye reacts so well to light that it could see the flame of a candle in absolute darkness from about 30 miles away.

Fact 230: During the nine seasons of "How I Met Your Mother" Ted dated 29 women who were not the mother.

Fact 231: The term "Internet" is the short form of the technical term "Internetwork", which was originally used for the technology at the time of its creation.

Fact 232: The Sapir-Whorf hypothesis states that the language a person speaks directly influences their way of thinking. Learning a new language could therefore change the way a person thinks about a problem.

Fact 233: During the Nuremberg Trials, a psychological test and an intelligence test were carried out on many accused Nazi functionaries and high-ranking military personnel. All Nazi leaders (except for Julius Streicher) displayed above-average intelligence, and some even had an IQ of 140. The former commander of the German Air Force, Hermann Göring, for example, had an IQ of 138.

Fact 234: The 1967 Space Treaty stipulates that no country has the right to annex or occupy a celestial body. At the same time, it prohibits the stationing of nuclear weapons in space or the establishment of a military base or military exercises on the moon. More than 100 states, including the USA and Russia, have signed this treaty.

Fact 235: The "Blue Java" banana is a special type of banana with a blue exterior and a slight vanilla taste.

Fact 236: In France there is a village named "Pussy".

Fact 237: The oxygen levels of a fetus in the womb are almost as low as on Mount Everest. The low oxygen level helps the fetus to sleep most of its time in the womb.

Fact 238: After a school class from Sarajevo had taken a field trip in 2014, it was discovered that seven girls were pregnant. To this day, the question of paternity has not been conclusively resolved.

Fact 239: There are more people in New York City with access to internet than people in Africa with internet connections.

Fact 240: In 200 million years, a day on Earth will last 25 hours.

Fact 241: Beavers have orange teeth, as they contain a lot of iron. The mineral makes the teeth particularly resistant to external forces.

Fact 242: Until the 1980s, flight attendants in the United States were required to be single. Getting married was even considered grounds for dismissal.

Fact 243: In the earth's core, there are temperatures of up to 10,800 degrees Fahrenheit.

Fact 244: When the historic Plaza Hotel in New York opened its doors in 1907, one night cost $2.50, which by today's standards would be about $64. Today, however, you have to pay more than $1,000 per night.

Fact 245: The mineral "Tanzanite" is a gemstone that is mined exclusively in the Gilewy Hills near Arusha in Tanzania. This makes the gems rarer than diamonds.

Fact 246: During the 1990s, software errors were the most common source of missile crashes in space travel. For example, the Ariane 5 rocket crashed in 1996 because the acceleration reading was stored as a 16-bit integer rather than a 32-bit integer.

Fact 247: In Paris there is only one stop sign.

Fact 248: The superhero "The Access" belongs to both DC and Marvel. He has the ability to open an inter-dimensional gate between both comic worlds.

Fact 249: In winter, the rotor blades of wind turbines are heated so that no ice forms on them.

Fact 250: The WWF chose a panda for its logo, in order to save print costs and to set a sign.

Fact 251: In addition to rainbows, there are also fogbows.

Fact 252: In 2005, Mark Zuckerberg offered Facebook for 75 million dollars to MySpace. The CEO of MySpace, Chris DeWolfe - declined.

Fact 253: In 2016, the first German championship in mermaid swimming was held. Both men and women pull a kind of tail fin over their legs, and their time over a certain distance is measured.

Fact 254: The national animal of Scotland is a unicorn.

Fact 255: Taiwan was the first country to provide free Wi-Fi to all citizens.

Fact 256: The Lotus Temple in India is open to everyone, regardless of their religion.

Fact 257: More than 50 percent of the world's population has never received a phone call.

Fact 258: One million seconds correspond to about twelve days, while one billion seconds correspond to 32 years.

Fact 259: The Vatican has its own telephone company, its own radio station, its own TV station, its own stamps, its own currency and its own army.

Fact 260: In 1991 Dubai had only one skyscraper. Today, there are more than 400.

Fact 261: Andorra does not have an army of its own. Instead, the law stipulates that at least every male head of household must possess a weapon for defense purposes. The law even obliges the police to make a weapon available to every male citizen who does not have one.

Fact 262: The development of chemical drugs can be traced back to the Nazis. For example, scientists in the Third Reich discovered an active substance that helped soldiers to march 55 miles without stopping.

Fact 263: The penis foreskin of burn patients can be used for healthy skin growth.

Fact 264: It takes an average employee at McDonald's about seven months to earn the amount the CEO makes in one hour.

Fact 265: Only five percent of all humans have red hair.

Fact 266: In its home market of South Korea, Samsung is more than just a tech company. A South Korean can be born in a Samsung-run hospital, live in a Samsung apartment, attend Samsung University and be buried by a Samsung funeral home.

Fact 267: A false pregnancy (scientific term: "pseudocyesis") is a mental illness in which the affected person shows all the symptoms of a pregnancy without actually being pregnant. In addition to the absence of menstruation, swelling of the breasts and abdomen can also occur. The disease is an example of how great the influence of the psyche can be on a human organism.

Fact 268: The Scottish kilt originally came from France.

Fact 269: On a flight from Amsterdam to Boston a woman from Uganda gave birth to a child. In the end, the baby was given Canadian citizenship as it was born in their airspace.

Fact 270: Martin Goodman - one of the founders of Marvel - thought Spider-Man was a bad idea because people do not like spiders.

Fact 271: A duel with three participants is called a truel.

Fact 272: Oskar Schindler died a poor man after spending his entire fortune protecting Jews from the Nazis. Of the approximately 15 million Jews worldwide, about 8,500 owe him their life. To this day, he is the only Nazi buried on Mount Zion in Israel.

Fact 273: In the 1960s, the Barbie model "Slumber Party Barbie" was released, which gave children extra tips on how to lose weight. One of them was that you should not eat anything.

Fact 274: The modern look of the U.S. flag was designed by a school child from Ohio as a school project. His teacher gave him a B-.

Fact 275: A dog's sense of smell is 10,000 times stronger than that of a human being.

Fact 276: The Jewish boxer Salamo Arouch was imprisoned in a concentration camp during World War II and was forced to fight against other inmates. The loser was shot or gassed.

Fact 277: The world's longest escalator is 453 feet long and located in St. Petersburg, Russia.

Fact 278: The International Space Station ISS is in orbit about 250 miles above the earth.

Fact 279: Chinatown in New York is the largest settlement of Chinese citizens outside Asia.

Fact 280: Measured by the number of units sold, the most successful video games of all time are Minecraft, Tetris and GTA 5.

Fact 281: With 133 days at sea, the Chinese Poon Lim holds the record for the longest time a shipwrecked person has spent alone on a raft on the high seas. During his time on the ocean, he even managed to kill a shark.

Fact 282: In Dubai people own refrigerator magnets, which order a pizza by pressing them.

Fact 283: The gigantism of the dinosaurs and many other prehistoric animal species can be traced back to epochs with a significantly increased oxygen concentration in the air. For example, the oxygen content in the Carboniferous was 35 percent instead of the current 21 percent.

Fact 284: On average, a person farts 14 times a day.

Fact 285: Celery has "negative" calories - it costs more energy to digest it.

Fact 286: To prove their credibility in court in early Rome, men have sworn on their balls.

Fact 287: A study concluded that people with a lower IQ more frequently tend to be more homophobic and racist than people with a higher IQ.

Fact 288: The average distance a man walks on foot during his life is four times around the world.

Fact 289: Historical finds prove that man sailed on ships as early as 6,000 years BC. The first traces of wheels, however, only date back to 4,000 years BC, meaning that ships seem to have been invented before the wheel.

Fact 290: When her husband died in the war in 1941, Ukrainian Marina Oktyabrskaya sold all her belongings and donated the money to the military to buy a tank. She was able to convince the military command to drive the tank herself and turned out to be an excellent tank driver. After she died in battle in 1944, she was posthumously awarded the title "Hero of the Soviet Union".

Fact 291: During World War II, a Canadian soldier smuggled his bear "Winnipeg" to Britain, and it later became an attraction at the London Zoo. Young Christopher Robin Milne loved this bear so much that he gave his teddy bear the same name. This in turn inspired his father to write the stories about the bear Winnie the Pooh.

Fact 292: All people begin their lives as females. The male Y chromosome becomes active just after the fifth week of gestation.

Fact 293: The average person watches their favorite movie 29 times in their lifetime.

Fact 294: During the Second World War a special event was held in a news magazine. Two soldiers were betting who would be the first to kill 100 enemy soldiers with a sword. Both died before they could win the competition.

Fact 295: The storming of the Bastille was mainly symbolic, at the time there were only nine prisoners who were subsequently freed.

Fact 296: The father of actor Robert Downey Jr. brought his son into contact with drugs at the early age of six. By the age of eight, he was already a drug addict.

Fact 297: There is a skeleton of a Tyrannosaurus Rex on the Google campus. It is supposed to remind employees not to let Google die out.

Fact 298: In 1970, roughly six billion dollars were spent on fast food. Nowadays, it is about 200 billion dollars.

Fact 299: The most popular quotes from Barney Stinson from "How I Met Your Mother" are "Have you met Ted?", "Wait for it", "What up" and "Suit up" and are already mentioned in the first episode of "How I Met Your Mother".

Fact 300: Although Japan has only one third of the population of the United States, more than six times as many Japanese people are more than 100 years old.

Fact 301: Because a big butt is a sign of fertility, men feel more attracted to women with larger butts.

Fact 302: A "Gish gallop" is a debating technique in which one's arguments consist essentially of half-truths and lies, so that it is impossible for the counterpart to refute all the falsehoods. The Gish gallop was named after the creationist Duane T. Gish.

Fact 303: In 2002, long-distance runner Tom Johnson competed against a horse in an 50-mile race. He ran the distance in five hours and 45 minutes, arriving ten seconds ahead of the horse.

Fact 304: In 1974, North Korea ordered 1,000 Volvo vehicles and other equipment worth 73 million euros from Sweden. To this day, North Korea has not paid for the shipment, and due to accumulated interest the debt has increased to more than 300 million euros.

Fact 305: Liechtenstein completed what was possibly the most successful military intervention in history. During World War I, the country sent a total of 80 soldiers to the Italian border. During their entire deployment, they hardly ever had to engage in military operations. After the end of the war, while marching back to their homeland, the soldiers made friends with an Austrian who came along back to Liechtenstein with them. So of the 80 soldiers deployed, 81 returned.

Fact 306: Based on a fan petition, LEGO launched the production of a special Big Bang theory set in 2015.

Fact 307: In 1993, Canadian lawyer Garry Hoy wanted to prove to a group of visitors that the glass in the Toronto Dominion Centre was unbreakable. To demonstrate this, he jumped against the glass - which thereupon broke out of its frame and plummeted downwards together with Garry Hoy. Hoy died, but the pane of glass remained intact, even after the fall.

Fact 308: Although Christopher Columbus was the first to discover the American continent, it was the Italian Amerigo Vespucci who came up with the idea that this might be a new continent and not an Indian island, as Columbus had initially thought. In memory of this insight, the continent was named "America" after Amerigo Vespucci.

Fact 309: Whenever the American President is outside the White House, a member of his security team carries a suitcase containing all the information and communications technology needed to authorize a nuclear attack. This is to enable the president to give orders for a military strike regardless of his location. The suitcase is therefore nicknamed the "Nuclear Football".

Fact 310: The composition of breast milk adapts to the age and thus to the needs of a child.

Fact 311: 6 out of the top 10 countries with the highest annual net loss of forested are can be found in Africa.

Fact 312: In 1925, Coca-Cola published a key pendant in the shape of a swastika.

Fact 313: One study documents that many people, after two years of obtaining their tertiary qualifications, remember only ten percent of the content they have learned.

Fact 314: Fifty Shades of Grey began as erotic fan fiction about the main characters of Twilight: Bella and Edward.

Fact 315: French was the national language of Great Britain for more than 300 years.

Fact 316: During the shooting of "The Wolf of Wall Street", actor Jonah Hill had to receive medical treatment after contracting bronchitis due to the excessive intake of fake cocaine.

Fact 317: Japanese people believe that black cats bring good luck.

Fact 318: Eminem's mother sued the rapper because he insulted her several times in his songs. She received damages of 1,600 dollars.

Fact 319: From 1920 onwards, Alexander Alexandrovich Bogdanov tried to discover a medical fountain of youth by performing blood transfusions on himself and injecting himself with the blood of younger people. One blood transfusion, however, was contaminated with malaria and tuberculosis, which eventually killed Bogdanov.

Fact 320: In 1889, the pharmaceutical company Bayer sold the drug diacetylmorphine, which was marketed as a remedy for morphine addicts. Nowadays, the drug is better known as "heroin".

Fact 321: It was only in 1990 that the World Health Organization (WHO) officially ceased to regard homosexuality as a mental illness.

Fact 322: The largest bomb ever detonated was tested by the United States in 1954 and had an explosive power equivalent to a thousand times that of the Hiroshima nuclear bomb. After the test, the scientists found that the bomb had almost twice the explosive force they had previously calculated. The flash was seen 250 miles away, and radiation injuries occurred within a radius of more than 87 miles.

Fact 323: The farthest distance a sniper met his target is 3,540 meters and was set up by a Canadian elite soldier. The projectile flew about ten seconds through the air.

Fact 324: Contraceptive pills also work for gorillas.

Fact 325: In terms of the assessment of one's own personal satisfaction, people are most unhappy at the age of 55.

Fact 326: After a 19 year old girl became the three millionth follower of Venezuelan President Hugo Chávez on Facebook, the president gave her a house.

Fact 327: When you immerse yourself in water, your breathing stops automatically, your heart rate slows down and the blood increasingly migrates from your hands and feet into your upper body. This is referred to as the diving reflex, the exact cause of which has not yet been fully determined.

Fact 328: For his first role in Star Wars Episode 4, Han Solo actor Harrison Ford received $10,000 in 1977, while for Episode 7 in 2015 he was paid $20 million.

Fact 329: When a Fiat employee realized when the Google Street View car will record Södertälje in Sweden, he parked a Fiat in front of the Swedish Volkswagen headquarter to be present in Google Street View for the next years.

Fact 330: Jonah Falcon, the man with the longest penis in the world, was arrested at San Francisco airport because security people mistook his large penis for a bomb.

Fact 331: In Japan, there is an office tower in which a highway runs though, between the fifth and the seventh floors.

Fact 332: The role of the character Captain Jack Sparrow from "Pirates of the Caribbean" was originally given to Jim Carry. He refused as he rather wanted to make Bruce Almighty.

Fact 333: The police of Saudi Arabia have a special witches-unit, where people can report cases of magic. Fortune telling is also considered a crime.

Fact 334: On 24 January 1961 a US Air Force B-52 bomber crashed during a military exercise and had to initiate the emergency jettison of two hydrogen bombs over the Goldboro regaion (North Carolina, USA). On one of the bombs, only one of four safety devices remained intact after the crash, while the second bomb landed in a swamp area where remains of the bomb are still found to this day.

Fact 335: The official title of the British Prime Minister's cat is "Chief Mouser to the Cabinet Office".

Fact 336: The first cloned cat has been called "CC" as an abbreviation for "carbon copy"'.

Fact 337: The urine and sweat of people suffering from "leucinosis" smells of maple syrup. Those affected lack an enzyme needed to break down certain protein elements. For this reason, their bodies increasingly contain the degradation product "sotolone", which smells strongly of maple syrup.

Fact 338: Because of the reduced distance to the central core of the earth at the equator, people at the equator weigh less than people at the poles.

Fact 339: A building on the Amazon campus - the Wainwright Building - was named after the website's first customer.

Fact 340: In 2011, torero Juan José Padilla lost his left eye during a bullfight. Five years later, the one-eyed bullfighter was once again caught by a bull - in the same spot.

Fact 341: Scientists at the Chinese University of Hong Kong have shown that the protein lectin can help prevent the development of tumor cells, prevent viruses from multiplying, and even serve as the starting material for a cure for HIV. Since lectin is found in bananas and is responsible for the brown coloring of the fruit, the darkest bananas are therefore the healthiest.

Fact 342: "Steve Jobs" is the name of an Italian fashion label. The company behind the brand was founded in 2012 by two brothers after they had realized that Apple had never secured the rights to the name "Steve Jobs".

Fact 343: With over 1,200 different subspecies, bats account for about 20 percent of all known mammal species.

Fact 344: After beverage company Mountain Dew launched an online poll to suggest and vote on the name of a new drink, the ultimate favorites were "Hitler Did Nothing Wrong", "Gushing Granny" and "Fapple" (alluding to masturbation).

Fact 345: Human gastric acid is so corrosive that it could dissolve a razor blade.

Fact 346: The oldest ever found advertisement dates back to 3,000 BC and was found in the ruins of Thebes. It advertised a slave named Shem.

Fact 347: The saying "Happy wife, happy life" has been scientifically proven. Men whose wives are happy are also happier themselves.

Fact 348: There are more Subway restaurants worldwide than McDonald's outlets.

Fact 349: In 1957 a senior woman had to be brought out of a baseball stadium after being hit in her face by a baseball. When the paramedics were carrying her out, a second ball hit her.

Fact 350: The name "Africa" derives from the Latin name "Afri" which was used to refer to the inhabitants of then-known northern Africa.

Fact 351: Statistically, most cars are stolen on New Year's Day.

Fact 352: For every human eaten by a shark, 600,000 sharks are eaten by humans.

Fact 353: Since 1944, Iceland does not have its own army, and have not been attacked by other countries since.

Fact 354: Pizza is one of the few words that is understood almost everywhere in the world.

Fact 355: The first virtual reality cinema has already opened its doors in Amsterdam. Visitors can swivel their chairs to enjoy a 360-degree-view of the film.

Fact 356: The copyright to the song "Happy birthday to you" expired in 2016 in the USA and in 2017 in the European Union. Until then, royalties had to be paid to Warner Music whenever the song was played on radio or television or in a cinema.

Fact 357: Since 1987, the Chinese government has been sending plant seeds into space on a regular basis in order to deliberately cause mutations in the plants due to the increased radiation in space. The objective is to create improved and more productive plants. This project has already yielded giant eggplants, a 1.6 feet long cucumber and higher yielding pepper plants.

Fact 358: The Hungarian psychologist László Polgár put forward the theory that every human being can be educated to become a genius if only you start encouragement early enough. He convinced his wife of the idea and taught his three daughters chess at the age of four. All three daughters reached the rank of Grand Master. One of the daughters became the second-best female chess player in the world - behind her sister Judit Polgár, who even rose to become the world's best female chess player. Overall, she ranked eighth worldwide.

Fact 359: If you take the measure of anything, such as the height of a mountain, the length of a river or the price of a company's share, then the probability that this number begins with a one is about 30 percent. The probability of this number beginning with a nine, on the other hand, is only five percent. This phenomenon is known as "Benford's Law" and has frequently been used to disprove fake statistics.

Fact 360: The lyrebird is capable of perfectly imitating almost any sound it hears. Birds of this species have been observed imitating the sounds of a chainsaw, a gunshot, a camera shutter or even an explosion.

Fact 361: In the early 20th century the Irish woman Mary Mallon, known as "Typhoid Mary", became infected with typhoid fever and became the first person in the US to be infected with the bacterium, but not to fall ill with it. Due to her ignorance, she infected more than 100 people with the deadly disease and caused the death of several friends and acquaintances.

Fact 362: In preparation of the movie "Rocky" Sylvester Stallone asked the former professional boxer Earnie Shavers to beat him multiple times in the face at full force. Stallone vomited after his first punch.

Fact 363: Dogs and humans are the only mammals with a prostate.

Fact 364: Approximately 70 percent of the world's total oxygen is released by plants in the oceans.

Fact 365: Born in 1930, Irene Triplett is the last living descendant of a civil war veteran. Although the US civil war ended in 1865, she continues to receive her late father's veteran's pension of $73.13 every month. Her father Mose Triplett was only 18 years old when he went to war and 83 when Irene was born.

Fact 366: The symbol on the on/off button on remote controls - a circle crossed by a straight line - represents the two binary characters 0 and 1.

Fact 367: Uranus is 63 times larger than Earth.

Fact 368: An average pubic hair has a life expectancy of three weeks. A head hair "lives" in comparison up to seven years.

Fact 369: 60% of the African continent is covered by deserts and drylands.

Fact 370: It is assumed that the pizza Hawaii was invented in Canada.

Fact 371: Shakuntala Devi holds the world record in mental arithmetic. In 1980 a computer randomly chose the two 13-digit numbers 7,686,369,774,870 and 2,465,099,745,779, which Devi had to multiply. It took her only 28 seconds for the correct answer: 18,947,668,117,995,426,462,773,730!

Fact 372: Male ants have no fathers because unfertilized ant eggs always produce male ants and only fertilized eggs produce female ants.

Fact 373: NASA plans to grow crops on the moon in the next six years.

Fact 374: Before Africa was colonized by foreign powers it comprised up to 10,000 different states and autonomous groups. All of them had different languages and manners.

Fact 375: The election slogan "Yes we can" actually comes from "Bob the Builder".

Fact 376: According to physical calculations, trees can reach a maximum height of 426 feet.

Fact 377: Babies already dream in their mother's womb

Fact 378: Bill Gates has already donated more than 28 billion dollars since 2007. It is estimated that this has saved about six million lives.

Fact 379: In 1946, the United States made Denmark an offer to buy Greenland for 100 million dollars. However, the Danes refused.

Fact 380: Cleopatra was not an Egyptian, but originally came from Greece.

Fact 381: In Clark County, Nevada, there is a house that is an almost exact replica of the Simpson family house.

Fact 382: In 2016, Pizza Hut delivered a pizza to the top of Kilimanjaro, setting the world record for the highest pizza delivery ever.

Fact 383: One pound of muscles burns 16,300 calories per year.

Fact 384: It only takes one drop of engine oil to contaminate more than 25 liters of water.

Fact 385: American professional basketball player Shaquille O'Neal scored only a single three-point shot throughout his entire professional career.

Fact 386: From January 1st to December 31st of 1881, three different men - Rutherford B. Hayes, James A. Garfield and Chester A. Arthur - held the office of President of the United States.

Fact 387: According to estimates, the iPhone is the most profitable product in the world. About 50 percent of the selling price is Apple's profit.

Fact 388: Dogs have such a good sense of smell that they can even smell when a person's insulin level drops too low.

Fact 389: Barney Stinson from "How I Met Your Mother" has worn the ducky tie in 11 episodes.

Fact 390: About 20 percent of all calories consumed worldwide comes from rice.

Fact 391: Araucana chickens are also referred to as Easter egg chickens, because their eggs can be blue, green, red or brown.

Fact 392: The hawksbill turtle has probably existed since the Cretaceous period.

Fact 393: Within 29 weeks, Harry Truman rose from US Senator to Vice President of the United States and then to President of the United States before becoming the first man to order the launch of a nuclear bomb.

Fact 394: The Atlantic Ocean is saltier than the Pacific Ocean.

Fact 395: J. K. Rowling - the author of the Harry Potter books - is no longer a billionaire. She has donated most of her fortune.

Fact 396: Finland has hosted the official "Wife Carrying World Championship" since 1992. In this competition, men carry their wives as fast as possible over a long obstacle course. In the end, the winner receives his wife's weight in beer.

Fact 397: The founder of "Victoria's Secret" sold the company for a million dollars in 1982 and committed suicide in 1993 by jumping off the Golden Gate Bridge.

Fact 398: Pablo Escobar - the world's biggest drug lord - had so much cash that he had to spend 2,500 dollars a month on rubber bands that held his money together.

Fact 399: The area on earth, which is suitable for coffee plants to grow, is called the bean belt.

Fact 400: The seven wonders of the ancient world only existed concurrently for 60 years.

Fact 401: Bob Dylans real name is Robert Allen Zimmermann.

Fact 402: Scientist Daniel Fahrenheit wanted to avoid negative temperature values on his temperature scale, so he defined the lowest temperature he could artificially reach as zero degrees Fahrenheit.

Fact 403: Nearly 65 percent of all autistic people are left-handed.

Fact 404: In the United States, it is common to call "shotgun" if you want to sit in a car's front passenger seat. This term originated in the Wild West. In addition to mail, stagecoaches also carried valuables, so that attacks were frequent. For protection, the area to the right of the driver was occupied by a shotgunner. This is why the right front seat of a car continues to be called "shotgun" to this day.

Fact 405: According to the music magazine "Rolling Stone", the song "Like a Rolling Stone" by Bob Dylan is the best song of all times. Second place goes to "Satisfaction" by The Rolling Stones and third place to "Imagine" by John Lennon.

Fact 406: It is possible to die even 24 hours after drowning. People who die from "dry drowning" do not tend to notice their discomfort while the water continues to spread in their lungs until they die.

Fact 407: Transplanted testicles continue to produce the donor's sperm.

Fact 408: The original name of Starbucks was actually "Pequods".

Fact 409: Ransom payments to abductors can be written off as taxes in Germany.

Fact 410: In the United States, the term "public viewing" refers to a public coroner's examination.

Fact 411: Before she became famous, the singer "Pink" worked for McDonald's.

Fact 412: In the United States, it is a legal requirement that eggs be washed before sale. The EU, however, stipulates that eggs may not be washed before sale. Both laws were introduced to protect against salmonella.

Fact 413: Laughing one hundred times burns the same calories as a 15-minute workout on the bike.

Fact 414: There are butterflies that migrate south every winter, just like birds. Every autumn, the monarch butterfly sets off on its journey from the north of the United States to Mexico, covering a distance of 2,175 miles. Every day, they cover between 44 and 186 miles.

Fact 415: Canada owns about 20 percent of the world's fresh water.

Fact 416: Okinawa Island in Japan is the safest place in the world. More than 450 people, who are more than 100 years old, live there.

Fact 417: If you visit Rainymood.com you can hear the sounds of rain.

Fact 418: During a solar eclipse, it appears to observers on earth as if the sun and moon were exactly the same size. However, this is only a huge coincidence, because the sun is 400 times as big as the moon, but also 400 times further away.

Fact 419: The Greenland shark, among others, eats polar bears and deer.

Fact 420: Night vision devices display a green image because people can perceive the most amount of contrast in green.

Fact 421: The largest insect of all time lived 300 million years ago. Meganeura resembled today's dragonflies, but had an enormous wingspan of 30 inches.

Fact 422: US student Devin Gaines made headlines in 2007 when he succeeded in obtaining five Bachelor's degrees at the same time. However, he died just two months after receiving his degrees when he drowned in a river while bathing.

Fact 423: In 2015, a cow in Texas gave birth to quadruplets. For cows, the probability of such a birth is about one in 11.2 million. By the way, the names of the four calves are Eeny, Meeny, Miny and Moo.

Fact 424: The increased use of the drug "Sumatriptan" can lead to a green coloration of the blood.

Fact 425: One gram of DNA contains as much information as could be stored on 600 billion traditional CDs.

Fact 426: There are more people with obesity than malnutrition worldwide.

Fact 427: In 2012 a British man named Wesley Carrington bought a metal detector and within 20 minutes found gold from the Roman Age worth 100,000 pounds.

Fact 428: The explosion of a modern nuclear atomic bomb in London would produce such a large pressure wave that glass panes in Berlin would also shatter.

Fact 429: Vladimir Putin once tried to exploit Angela Merkel's fear of dogs. The two heads of state met in Sochi in January 2007 to discuss important issues related to energy policy and cooperation between Russia and the EU. During the entire conversation, Putin let his Labrador "Koni" stay close to Merkel's legs.

Fact 430: The mascot on the Pringles package is called "Julius Pringles".

Fact 431: At the age of five years and eleven months, Ayan Qureshi passed the "Microsoft Certified Professional Test", making him the youngest computer specialist in the world.

Fact 432: Koalas sleep about 90 percent of their lives.

Fact 433: At birth, a blue whale is already 26 feet long and weighs more than eight tons. In its first year, the newborn gains approximately 176 pounds of weight per day - 7.3 pounds per hour.

Fact 434: The world record for the most consecutive push-ups was set in 1980 by Minoru Yoshida from Japan who managed to do 10,507 in a row.

Fact 435: Before erasers were invented, bread was used to remove pencil traces.

Fact 436: The Sims was originally designed as an architecture simulator.

Fact 437: A chameleon's tongue can grow to up to one and a half times its body size.

Fact 438: Spending more than 15,000 dollars for a wedding increases the rate of divorce compared to couples who have a cheaper wedding.

Fact 439: The largest land animal permanently living in Antarctica is only 0.24 inches long. It is the wingless mosquito species "Belgica antarctica".

Fact 440: The IKEA catalogue is the only book on earth, of which there are more copies than the Bible.

Fact 441: For blind people, who are allergic to dog hair, there are blind horses. A special breed, who are extremely small and very tame.

Fact 442: More people know the logo of McDonald's than the Christian Cross.

Fact 443: In 2014, Red Bull spent a billion dollars on marketing, but only 600 million dollars on the production of beverages.

Fact 444: Leonardo da Vinci loved animals so much that he often bought caged animals to set them free.

Fact 445: The old president moves out and the new president moves into the White House during the inauguration ceremony, which lasts only a few hours.

Fact 446: The speculum - a tool for gynaecologists - was already used 1,300 years before Christ.

Fact 447: The largest industrial accident ever happened on 16 April 1947 in Texas City. While cargo was being loaded, 2,200 tons of ammonium nitrate ignited on the ship Grandcamp in city's port. The explosion was so massive that even at a distance of ten miles, people were knocked off their feet, and window panes burst as far as 37 miles away. 581 people died as a result of the explosion and over 8,400 people were injured.

Fact 448: The phenomenon of having to sneeze when suddenly exposed to bright light is called the photic sneeze reflex.

Fact 449: In 2012 about 37 percent of Italians had never used the Internet.

Fact 450: In 1647 Christmas was forbidden by the English Parliament.

Fact 451: Alcohol protects against radiation.

Fact 452: The South African currency "Rand" derives its name from the mountain range "Witwatersrand" in South Africa. The area is known for its numerous gold deposits, which brought the country great prosperity.

Fact 453: Twitter's ticker symbol is TWTR. However, due to a mix-up on the first trading day of the short message service's shares, a lot of stock traders bought the shares of Tweeter's Home Entertainment with the ticker symbol TWTRQ, boosting the share price of the small company by 2,200 percent.

Fact 454: The grapefruit was actually an accident. It was developed by chance from a cross between pomelos and oranges.

Fact 455: In the movie "Halloween" the villain Michael Myers wears a mask. In order to save production costs, they bought a Captain Kirk mask and simply painted it over.

Fact 456: In ancient Rome, urine was used for leather tanning and in laundries. The business with urine prospered so much that Emperor Vespasian even levied a urine tax. He justified the tax to his son Titus by holding the money under his nose and asking him if it smelled bad. When his son answered no, Vespasian famously said "Atqui e lotio est" (And yet it comes from urine). Over time, this developed into the phrase "Pecunia non olet" (money does not stink).

Fact 457: Goats have rectangular pupils.

Fact 458: Google uses camels with a camera attached in the desert to get images for Google Street View.

Fact 459: In Sri Lanka, killing an elephant is punishable by death.

Fact 460: Gottfried Svartholm, a co-founder of Pirate Bay, let his mother read instructions for using computer programs to him at the age of six, in order to learn the basics of programming.

Fact 461: It has been scientifically proven that chicken soup is effective against colds. It blocks certain white blood cells that are partly responsible for inflammatory processes and are released in large quantities during infections. In addition, the protein cysteine contained in the soup has an anti-inflammatory and decongestant effect on the mucous membranes.

Fact 462: The first flags of pirates were red, not black.

Fact 463: If one took all the world's water and placed it into a cube, it would accommodate 39,375 cubic feet.

Fact 464: The album "Hybrid Theory" by Linkin Park is the most sold debut album of the 21st century.

Fact 465: The author J. K. Rowling was the first person in the world who became a billionaire by selling books.

Fact 466: Between 2009 and 2012, Alexander Bychkow killed and ate at least nine people. According to him, he did this to impress his ex-girlfriend, who had ended the relationship prior to the killings.

Fact 467: Four percent of all people do not fold their toilet paper, but scrunch it together instead.

Fact 468: Sneezing too intensively can cause a broken rib.

Fact 469: In 2011, scientists flew 100 paper planes from a height of 23 miles above Germany. Some of these paper planes have been found in Canada, USA, Australia and South America.

Fact 470: A study came to the conclusion that women are more attractive to men when they do not use make-up.

Fact 471: Gray whales exclusively mate in a threesome.

Fact 472: The word "idiot" is a psychology term that describes people with an IQ between 0 and 25.

Fact 473: The Swedish word for stepmother is "Bonusmamma".

Fact 474: Carrots were purple until the 17th century. The orange color is only a specially cultivated form that has prevailed over the past few centuries.

Fact 475: During the day, clouds are higher up in the sky than during the night.

Fact 476: From 1912 to 1948 architecture was an Olympic discipline.

Fact 477: In Italy, a man left his cat an inheritance of about ten million Euros.

Fact 478: The Diomedes Islands are a group of islands in the Arctic Ocean. The western island of this group belongs to Russia, while the eastern island belongs to the USA. Both islands are only 2.5 miles apart, but as the International Date Line runs between them, they are separated by a 21-hour time difference.

Fact 479: The longest boxing match in the world took place on 6 April 1893 between Andy Bowen and Jack Burke. The fight went on for 110 rounds and lasted for more than seven hours. In the end, both fighters were too tired and exhausted to keep on fighting.

Fact 480: Jonah Falcon has the biggest penis in the world. It has a length of almost 14 inches.

Fact 481: The first Twitter user to reach more than a million followers was Ashton Kutcher.

Fact 482: In 2016, in an experiment, a monkey succeeded in moving a wheelchair in which it was sitting through its thoughts alone.

Fact 483: Samsung is responsible for 20 percent of South Korea's gross domestic product.

Fact 484: The ISS orbits the Earth at a speed of 4.76 miles per second.

Fact 485: The average starting salary for a developer at Microsoft is 106,000 dollars.

Fact 486: Buzz Aldrin was the first person to have a bowel movement on the moon.

Fact 487: Apple owns more cash than the United States.

Fact 488: Sharks were on the earth before trees existed.

Fact 489: The long drink "gin and tonic" was invented by the British in the 17th century as protection against malaria. The reason for this is that until 1940, the quinine contained in tonic water was the only substance known to be effective against malaria. However, since this also causes the tonic water to taste bitter, the drink was mixed with gin to improve its taste.

Fact 490: Terminator 2, The Silence of the Lambs, The Beauty and the Beast and the Prince of Bel Air are closer in time to the moon landing than on today's date.

Fact 491: 30% of Earth's remaining mineral resources can be found in Africa.

Fact 492: On the distant planet HD 189733b it rains molten glass at wind speeds of 4,350 miles per hour.

Fact 493: The Victoria Falls are the largest waterfall in Africa. Its high is 355 feet (108 metres).

Fact 494: At the age of 17, young Pattie Mellette got pregnant and was forced to have an abortion by her parents. She refused. Her child is Justin Bieber.

Fact 495: According to the Bible, the chicken came before the egg (Genesis 1:20-22).

Fact 496: Even blind people have optical hallucinations after taking LSD. However, this only occurs in those who have lost their vision during their lifetime.

Fact 497: The abbreviation "OMG" (oh my God) was first mentioned in 1917 in a letter to the former Prime Minister of Great Britain, Winston Churchill.

Fact 498: Because people born blind smile from birth, scientists have concluded that smiling is a genetically determined behavior which is not learned.

Fact 499: Angola has more Portuguese speaking people than Portugal.

Fact 500: Eight out of ten people who have been struck by lightning are male.

Fact 501: A statistician at Stanford University has already won the lottery four times and has received over 20 million dollars.

Fact 502: With an estimated fortune of around 23 billion dollars, Ingvar Kamprad, the founder of Ikea, was one of the richest people in the world. However, people close to him say that he still took the bus, lived in a small house and only ever booked economy flights.

Fact 503: One side effect of aspirin is headache.

Fact 504: The more intelligent one is, the more zinc and copper can be found in one's hair.

Fact 505: The most common languages in Africa are Arabic, English, Swahili, French, Berber, Hausa, Portuguese and Spanish.

Fact 506: The TV series "Breaking Bad" tells the story of chemistry teacher Walter White, who becomes the largest producer of methamphetamine (meth) in the entire southwest of the United States. There is, in fact, a real Walter White who claims to have cooked the best meth in Alabama for ten years. He, too, first produced the meth in a camping vehicle. His marriage broke apart because of his criminal dealings, and at times he was denied contact with his two children. Today he is in prison.

Fact 507: The entire human population could live in New Zealand, and the population density would still be lower than that of Manhattan in New York.

Fact 508: Hans Zimmer has composed the soundtracks for "Lion King", "Gladiator", "Pirates of the Caribbean", "Inception" and for the "Dark Night" trilogy. According to him he had spent two weeks in a music class during his childhood and learned the rest by himself.

Fact 509: Adolf Hitler's nephew William Patrick Hitler emigrated to the USA in 1939 and even fought alongside the Americans against Nazi Germany during the Second World War. He was even awarded the Purple Heart for his accomplishments during the war. After the war, however, he changed his name to William Patrick Stuart-Houston.

Fact 510: Philip Noel-Baker so far is the only person to have won both an Olympic medal and a Nobel Prize.

Fact 511: The Golden Gate Bridge is made up of so many wire ropes that put together they would circle the earth three times.

Fact 512: In ancient Greece, there was a system that allowed any citizen to start a vote to send individual politicians into exile for ten years.

Fact 513: In the history of the United States there have been 17 Americans who ran a marathon in less than two hours and ten minutes. In October 2011 this was achieved by 32 Kenyans.

Fact 514: The Marvel superhero Northstar, a French-Canadian mutant, was the first gay superhero in the world.

Fact 515: In his youth, Che Guevara boasted to not have washed his T-shirt for at least 25 weeks.

Fact 516: It is impossible to draw a six while turning your foot clockwise simultaneously.

Fact 517: Even though he is already dead, Michael Jackson has earned more than 100,000,000 dollars per year in the last seven years. In monetary terms, his most successful year was 2016, when he earned a total of over 825,000,000 dollars.

Fact 518: From 1781 to 1850, the planet Uranus was named George.

Fact 519: The "spotlight effect" describes the phenomenon of people often imagining that other people are paying much more attention to them than they actually do.

Fact 520: Athlete Mark Henry currently holds the world record in "5-Lift-Total". His personal records in the five disciplines of weightlifting (snatch, clean and jerk, squat, bench press and deadlift) total 3,257.3 pounds, making him officially the strongest person ever to live.

Fact 521: Retweets and Hashtags were not invented by Twitter, but were developed by users of the short message service and later integrated into the service as official functions.

Fact 522: When Facebook went public, it was worth more than eBay, Yahoo, Groupon, LinkedIn, Netflix and AOL combined.

Fact 523: In 1867 the USA bought Alaska from Russia for just 7.2 million dollars.

Fact 524: Cigarette filters do not change color during smoking because they retain pollutants, but rather because they are specifically designed to change their color. Studies have shown that because of the change in color, smokers feel that smoking with a filter is healthier than smoking without a filter and therefore smoke more.

Fact 525: With a total length of about 4,132 miles (6,650 kilometres) the Nile River is the longest river in the world.

Fact 526: Nepal is the only country in the world that does not have a rectangular flag.

Fact 527: The name of the Microsoft search engine "Bing" comes from the word "Bingo", which you shout out when you get exactly the answer you had hoped for.

Fact 528: The younger you look for your age, the higher the likelihood to live for a long time.

Fact 529: Pigs cannot see to the sky.

Fact 530: Leonardo DiCaprio was named after Leonardo da Vinci. His mother was looking at a drawing by the artist in a museum, when she felt young Leonardo move for the first time.

Fact 531: Just like whales, elephants and hippos can communicate with their fellow creatures over long distances via infrasound.

Fact 532: In 1911, the Niagara Falls froze completely.

Fact 533: When the Mona Lisa was stolen from the Louvre in 1911, Pablo Picasso was one of the suspects.

Fact 534: It is assumed that so far only four percent of our oceans have been explored.

Fact 535: In Mumbai you can take out insurance against dodging paying of fares.

Fact 536: Angela Merkel's middle name is Dorothea.

Fact 537: Only two people have ever visited the lowest point on earth: the Mariana Trench. It is 36,201 feet below sea level. In contrast, twelve people have already been on the moon.

Fact 538: Facebook pays for all private flights taken by Mark Zuckerberg and his family. The cost amounts to 1.2 million dollars per year.

Fact 539: Monowi in Nebraska has only one inhabitant and he is also mayor of the city.

Fact 540: On the occasion of the new Star Wars Movie "The Force Awakens" the weirdest products were sold under the "Star Wars" trade mark. Including a knife block, oranges, mascara and special "Yoda water".

Fact 541: There are no reported incidents of death by dehydration in the history of world running. But there are plenty of cases of people dying because of drinking to much water.

Fact 542: The Italian state of Bellagio, namesake of the Las Vegas hotel with the same name, has fewer inhabitants than the hotel has rooms.

Fact 543: Ice cream manufacturer Ben & Jerry's has a cemetery for discontinued ice cream varieties on its premises.

Fact 544: According to current estimates, there are only three living Northern white rhinos left. So the species is on the verge of extinction.

Fact 545: As traffic in Bangkok has become so bad, the city has started to train special mobile obstetricians to help women give birth when they cannot make it to hospital on time.

Fact 546: The parrot "Alex" remains the only animal to ever have asked a question. When he was shown a mirror, he asked, "What color?"

Fact 547: The brain growth of early humans only began due to the increased protein intake from an increasingly meat-oriented diet.

Fact 548: Blind people have nightmares, and have them four times more often than normal seeing people do.

Fact 549: In Lapland, the horns of reindeers are sprayed with reflective color so that they can be seen better in the dark and car accidents can be prevented.

Fact 550: The teeth of limpets are the hardest biological material in the world.

Fact 551: The PlayStation 1 controller sold in North America was about ten percent larger than the controller sold in Japan, as Japanese people on average have smaller hands than North Americans.

Fact 552: The original name of the movie "Scream" was "Scary movie".

Fact 553: Scientists believe they have discovered an evolutionary jump. It was discovered that the Australian lizard stems from an egg-laying species to a viviparous one.

Fact 554: The two most common reasons for a bad temper are hunger and insufficient sleep.

Fact 555: The term "Checkmate" comes from the Persian phrase "Shah Mat" which means "the king is dead"

Fact 556: The record for "The most orgasms in one hour" is 134 for women and 16 for men.

Fact 557: The Australian prisoner Joseph Bolitho Johns broke out of prison so often that the police built a special prison cell for him. He also broke out of this.

Fact 558: The indents on a golf ball are called "dimples".

Fact 559: The Japanese word "karate" means "empty hand".

Fact 560: The most economically unprofitable movie in U.S. history is "ZYZZXD Road". It earned a total of 20 dollars.

Fact 561: Toilet paper was invented in China in the 13th century.

Fact 562: Thanks to a language computer, Stephen Hawking could speak at a rate of one word per minute.

Fact 563: The kidnapping of four-year-old Charley Ross in 1874 is considered to be the first kidnapping in the history of the USA to have been widely reported in the media. The girl, who would never be found, was lured by two men with fireworks and sweets. Due to the worldwide interest in this case, children are still advised not to accept sweets from strangers to this day.

Fact 564: From 200 decibels, music can be fatal, because then the air vesicles in your lung can burst.

Fact 565: Frederic Baur developed the boxing of Pringles Chips. After his death in 2008, his ashes were buried in a Pringles box.

Fact 566: Fully-grown bears can run as fast as horses.

Fact 567: The actor Nicolas Cage has already purchased his own grave. It is a pyramid several meters high in New Orleans.

Fact 568: When her ship capsized in 1880, the former queen of Thailand, Sunandha Kumariratana, drowned together with her daughter. Despite the presence of many courtiers, no one dared to save the queen, as just a few years earlier it had been punishable by death to touch a member of the royal family.

Fact 569: According to surveys among US prisoners, cigarettes are no longer the accepted currency behind bars, but ramen noodles.

Fact 570: The beginnings of the Internet date back to 1969, when US universities and the military networked mainframes to make more efficient use of their computing power. It was not until 1990 that the Internet was made accessible to the general public.

Fact 571: The "Like" button on Facebook was originally supposed to be called the "Awesome" button.

Fact 572: People cry the amount it would take to fill one bath tub in their whole life.

Fact 573: The city with the longest name in the world is Llanfairpwllgwyngyllgogerychwyrndrobwllllantysiliogogog och and is located in Wales.

Fact 574: A study conducted by Oxford University in 2009 showed that playing Tetris after a traumatic event can significantly improve trauma management.

Fact 575: It is estimated that about 70 percent of all Sicilian businesses pay protection money to the mafia. The average amount of the payment is between 200 and 5,000 euros. As a result, the Sicilian mafia Cosa Nostra supposedly takes in ten billion euros every year.

Fact 576: There is a real superhero in Tokyo. He calls himself Mangetsu Man and wears a purple bodysuit as well as a large yellow mask. He has made it his mission to rid the city of garbage and keep it clean.

Fact 577: The "S" in the name of Harry S. Truman only represents an "S".

Fact 578: The flightless terror birds were the direct descendants of the dinosaurs and ruled the earth 49 million years ago. This was the only time that birds ruled the world. The animals were up to ten feet tall and weighed up to 772 pounds. Their giant razor-sharp beak secured them a place at the top of the food chain for a long time.

Fact 579: The second name of Richard Nixon was Milhouse.

Fact 580: High heels were originally worn by men to look taller. It was only in the 17th century that women began to wear such shoes in order to be more masculine. The result was that men were no longer wearing high heels, so as not to look feminine.

Fact 581: US soldier John J. Kelly is the last person to receive the Medal of Honor twice. During World War I, he ran to the front line, destroyed a machine gun base, killed the artillerist with a grenade, shot a man with his pistol and rescued eight prisoners. He was only 19 years old at the time.

Fact 582: With a maximum speed of 68 miles per hour, the marlin is the fastest fish in the world. For comparison, a cruise ship travels the seas at an average speed of 19 miles per hour.

Fact 583: When the pirate Jean Lafitte learnt about a bounty on his head of 500 dollars was issued by the governor, he issued a bounty on the governor's head of 5,000 dollars.

Fact 584: There are still about 30 to 40 million people who move around as nomadic peoples without a permanent residence. In Mongolia, 40 percent of the population belong to this group.

Fact 585: In New York City, 6,000 people die every year as a result of obesity.

Fact 586: The spider species "Caeristris darwini"spins the largest webs in the world. Their size can reach more than ten feet.

Fact 587: There is a low probability that women can become pregnant a second time during pregnancy. This so-called phenomenon of "superfetation" is highly unlikely, but nevertheless possible. The last known case of a woman who was pregnant twice at the same time occurred in 2009.

Fact 588: The croissant is not a French creation, but an Austrian creation.

Fact 589: From a statistical point of view, women are the better drivers, as they cause less accidents.

Fact 590: The majority of astronauts, U.S. Presidents and Nobel Prize winners were first-borns.

Fact 591: Stephen Hawking had surpassed the life expectancy estimated by doctors by more than 50 years.

Fact 592: A Geiger counter clicks when it is exposed to radioactivity because the radiation releases electrons from the noble gas in the counter tube. This causes a chain reaction, resulting in a brief flow of electrical current, which is made audible via a loudspeaker.

Fact 593: The Flynn effect describes the fact that the average IQ increases with each generation. However, it is not clear why we humans are becoming more and more intelligent.

Fact 594: Although Cape Town is the southernmost city in Africa its not the southernmost point in the continent. That's Cape Agulhas which is roughly 100 miles (170km) southeast from Cape Town.

Fact 595: There are no one- and two-cent coins in Finland. Prices must always be rounded up or down to the nearest five cents by law.

Fact 596: The term "to google" was added to the Oxford English Dictionary in June 2006. It was defined as "Search for information about (someone or something) on the Internet using the search engine Google."

Fact 597: In Turkey there is a city called "Batman".

Fact 598: Humans and dolphins are the only animals, which have sex solely for pleasure.

Fact 599: If all the ships currently in service in the world were to sink, the sea level would fall minimally and not rise, as one might intuitively think.

Fact 600: Eminem repeated the ninth grade - three times.

Fact 601: For car races, Nissan only uses the number 23 on their vehicles, since in Japanese number two is pronounced as "ni" and three as "san". Together this gives "ni-san".

Fact 602: When Chinese basketball player Yao Ming first appeared for his new team in Houston, it was celebrated with 8,000 fortune cookies which were distributed to the fans. Ming was more than surprised, as he had never seen a fortune cookie in his life, as fortune cookies are not a Chinese, but an American invention.

Fact 603: Like humans, ducks have different accents.

Fact 604: Tesla founder Elon Musk barely escaped death in 2000 after contracting malaria in Brazil.

Fact 605: In 1967, Lawrence Roberts, one of the forefathers of the Internet, was still of the opinion that the exchange of messages among network participants was not an important motive for building a network of computers. Today, services such as WhatsApp, Telegram and e-mail have become an indispensable part of our everyday lives.

Fact 606: Henry Ford was the first tycoon to not let his employees work on Saturdays and Sundays, so that they could spend more time with their cars. Thus the weekend was born.

Fact 607: The deaf cannot get seasick.

Fact 608: The larvae of cicada of the genus Magicicada hatch only 17 years after they have been deposited in the ground and then live for only a few weeks. As a result, the United States are practically invaded by the small insects every 17 years.

Fact 609: The "Fallen Astronaut Sculpture" is the only work of art on the moon so far. It was created by Belgian artist Paul Van Hoeydonck and brought to the moon during the Apollo 15 mission in 1971. It commemorates the 14 astronauts who died prior to the Apollo 15 mission.

Fact 610: The country with the lowest population density is Mongolia. On average, there are only 4.9 people per square mile.

Fact 611: It has been scientifically proven that your nose actually grows when you lie. Scientists refer to this as the "Pinocchio effect".

Fact 612: If you multiply any integer by nine and then add the digits of the resulting number until there is only one digit left, you will end up with nine again.

Fact 613: With an estimated length of 221 feet, the Patagotitan mayorum was probably the longest dinosaur in the world. Weighing in at about 77 tons, it was as heavy as a Boeing 747 and therefore probably the heaviest land creature of all time.

Fact 614: Female kangaroos have three vaginas.

Fact 615: Male kangaroos flex their biceps to impress females.

Fact 616: The fuel of a Nazi V2 rocket was produced from 33 tons of potatoes – so-called potato schnapps.

Fact 617: In Japan, there is a road system where music is played when a car drives at the right speed.

Fact 618: After blue street lighting was introduced in some areas of Scotland and Japan, the suicide and crime rate dropped dramatically.

Fact 619: Fashion designer Ralph Lauren's real name is Ralph Lifshitz. At the age of 16, he decided to change his name because he didn't want the word "shit" to appear in his name.

Fact 620: The name "Lego" is derived from "Leg Godt", which means "play well" in Danish.

Fact 621: The Make-A-Wish-Foundation collects money to fulfil the dreams of seriously ill children.

Fact 622: "Fibrodysplasia ossificans progressiva" (abbreviated "FOP") is a rare disease in which the affected person slowly petrifies while still alive. The disease converts healthy muscle, connective and supporting tissue into bone material.

Fact 623: American school buses are yellow because a study from the 1930s showed that people can perceive the color yellow from a very long distance and therefore the risk of the school buses being involved in accidents decreases.

Fact 624: There are approximately sever million tons of plastic waste in our oceans. Just by doing without plastic bags, people could significantly improve the situation.

Fact 625: The only Spanish speaking country in Africa is Equatorial Guinea.

Fact 626: At the Marine Mammal Studies Institute, dolphins have been trained to get the audiences waste out of the basin. Each time they hand out trash to the animal attendants, they get food for it.

Fact 627: Afrikaans is the youngest language in the world. It was not officially recognized as an independent language until 1925.

Fact 628: The human brain consumes about 20 percent of the body's total energy.

Fact 629: The human heart beats more than 100,000 times a day.

Fact 630: The deepest species ever found is the devil worm (Halicephalobus mephisto). It was discovered in a cave in South Africa 2.2 miles underground.

Fact 631: The "carpet alarm clock" is a small carpet with an integrated alarm clock. The alarm can only be turned off by getting out of bed and putting your feet on the carpet.

Fact 632: Translated into Spanish "Colgate" means "hang yourself".

Fact 633: At the beginning of the 20th century, in the United States, it was possible to send one's own children to close relatives or friends by mail. The first known case of a child being sent by mail was an unidentified boy from Ohio, who in January 1913 was sent to his grandmother by his parents. The longest distance over which a child was sent by mail was approximately 75 miles. However, the children were never put inside a parcel. Instead, they were delivered directly to the post office and there entrusted to a postal employee who would then accompany them on their journey.

Fact 634: In the 18th century the Briton Mary Toft became famous for giving birth to rabbits. Years later she was sentenced to death when it became clear that she just put dead rabbits in her vagina, which she pushed out later on.

Fact 635: There are about nine million people in a prison around the world. 25 percent of them come from the USA.

Fact 636: February 29 was first introduced as a leap day by Julius Caesar in 45 BC.

Fact 637: Researchers at the Massachusetts Institute of Technology have developed a method that uses laser to transmit voice messages directly into the recipient's ear. So far, transmissions over a distance of 8.2 feet are reportedly possible.

Fact 638: When rebels stormed the home of Muammar al-Gaddafi, they discovered a photo album with pictures of the former U.S. Secretary of State Condoleezza Rice.

Fact 639: In 1968 Kip "Keino" almost arrived late to the Olympic 1,500 meter run, due to a traffic jam. He therefore left the car, ran the remaining 2.5 miles to the stadium and took home the gold medal.

Fact 640: Carde is the roman god for door handles, door sills and door hinges.

Fact 641: The Tetris effect, or Tetris syndrome, is the phenomenon that occurs when a person spends so much time on an activity that it affects all of their thinking, visual perception and even their dreams. So people who have played too much Tetris often dream of falling blocks or try to bring more order into all areas of their lives.

Fact 642: The world record for wearing the most underpants at the same time is at 302 pairs.

Fact 643: The Morse code is named after the inventor of the telegraph, Samuel Morse.

Fact 644: Approximately 200,000 new people are born each day.

Fact 645: Yellow teeth are more robust than white teeth.

Fact 646: On average, a man ejaculates 7,200 times during his entire life.

Fact 647: When being asked for his IQ, Stephen Hawking answered: "I have no idea. People who boast about their IQ are losers"

Fact 648: Due to more accurate methods in GPS surveying, the official size of Liechtenstein in Europe was corrected by 10,760 square feet in 2014.

Fact 649: There are approximately 80 species of fungi worldwide that can glow in the dark. This attracts insects, which then spread the spores of the fungus.

Fact 650: The entire border between the United States and Canada consists of a cleared strip of forest with a width of approximately 20 feet.

Fact 651: Google co-founders Sergey Brin and Larry Page originally named Google "Backrub". It was released in August 1996 and renamed to "Google" in 1997.

Fact 652: According to Amazon, the best-selling books on Kindle are the Bible, the Steve Jobs biography and the Hunger Games trilogy.

Fact 653: There's only one country between Finland and North Korea: Russia.

Fact 654: John Paul Stapp was a Brazilian researcher who investigated the effects of speed and acceleration on the human body. During an experiment carried out in 1954, he accelerated to 632 miles per hour before braking completely in 1.4 seconds. During this experiment, he was subject to 46.2 times the force of gravity. To this date, this is the highest acceleration a person has ever voluntarily withstood.

Fact 655: All books in Dumbledore's library in the Harry Potter films are actually telephone books, which have been remodeled to look like old books.

Fact 656: The average Bugatti customer owns 84 different vehicles, three airplanes and a yacht.

Fact 657: The drug carfentanyl is considered to be 5,000 times stronger than heroin. The substance was originally used to anaesthetize elephants, but it is increasingly being used by humans as a drug.

Fact 658: If you were able to fold a piece of paper a total of 102 times, it would be about as thick as the entire known universe.

Fact 659: The human brain needs 33 milliseconds to determine the mood of a person, from their facial expressions alone.

Fact 660: In remembrance of the deceased actor Paul Walker, Vin Diesel named his daughter "Pauline".

Fact 661: The Soviet Union had its own top-level domain. Until the collapse of the nation, there was a time window of 15 months during which it was possible to register domains with the ending ".su".

Fact 662: Almost 90% of all cases or malaria worldwide occur in Africa.

Fact 663: Actor Steve Buscemi (Armageddon, Boardwalk Empire) was a firefighter from 1980 to 1984. After the events of 9/11, he volunteered and worked unpaid twelve-hour shifts for over a week to support the New York Fire Department.

Fact 664: When Alexander Graham Bell, the inventor of the telephone, died in 1922, all telephones in the United States and Canada were switched off for one minute on 4 August of that year.

Fact 665: Most people are born in August.

Fact 666: The scientist Charles Darwin married his own cousin in 1839.

Fact 667: On 1 April 2017, Pornhub played a very special April fool's prank on its users. After they had clicked on a video, a picture with the message "Thanks for Sharing - Pornhub now has automatic video sharing to your social media accounts" was displayed.

Fact 668: Thioacetone is considered the world's worst smelling chemical. According to reports, when parts of the substance were released from a production site in Freiburg in 1889, it was reported that within a radius of 2,460 feet passers-by suddenly had to vomit because of the unbearable smell.

Fact 669: A horizontal line above a mathematical expression, for example to express an infinite period, is called a "vinculum".

Fact 670: In order for ketchup to pass the quality control of the manufacturing company Heinz, it must run out of the bottle at a speed of 0.28 miles per hour. If the ketchup runs out of the bottle faster or slower, its viscosity (thickness) is not correct and it is therefore not sold.

Fact 671: The Sahara is not just the largest desert in the world but also bigger than mainland USA.

Fact 672: If you enter "Beam me up, Scotty" as a search term on YouTube, all videos are "beamed" to the screen.

Fact 673: If you keep on walking north long enough, you will eventually be walking south. If, however, you keep on walking east, you will never be moving west.

Fact 674: After the death of Leonardo da Vinci, King Franz I. of France hung up the Mona Lisa in his bathroom.

Fact 675: The human heartbeat changes when listening to music and adapts to the sound.

Fact 676: The word "idiot" comes from the Greek word "idiotes" and originally referred to people who kept out of public political affairs.

Fact 677: On average, people laugh ten times a day.

Fact 678: Hulk originally was meant to be a grey monster but as the printing works had problems to always use the identical shade of grey, the creators decided to turn Hulk green.

Fact 679: The largest crossroads in the world is in China. It runs over five levels, has 20 exits and covers 99 acres.

Fact 680: Dwayne "The Rock" Johnson has a cousin - Tanoai Reed - who has a similar physique as the actor and also resembles him fairly closely in the face. Because of this, he has been his stunt double in all his movies for over 13 years.

Fact 681: The X-Men No. 1 is the best-selling comic book in the world with a total of eight million copies sold.

Fact 682: Sea water has an average salt content of 3.5 percent.

Fact 683: Manohar Aich won Mr. Universe in 1952. He got more than 100 years old and exercised regularly at the gym until he died.

Fact 684: The moonwalk was not actually invented by Michael Jackson. Cab Calloway included similar movements in his performances as early as 1932. At that time, however, people called it "The Buzz".

Fact 685: On 27 July, Finland celebrates "National Sleepy Head Day". There is a tradition that the last person in a household to wake up in the morning of this day is thrown into a cold lake.

Fact 686: There are more people living in California than in Canada.

Fact 687: The term "skyscraper" was originally a maritime term used for the highest mast on a sailing ship.

Fact 688: There is a type of jellyfish which is immortal.

Fact 689: After Christmas, Halloween is the holiday generating the highest sales revenues in the United States.

Fact 690: Half of the memory unit "byte", is known as a nibble.

Fact 691: David Hasselhoff secured the rights to his nickname "The Hoff" and the phrase "Do not Hassel the Hoff" as part of his divorce settlement.

Fact 692: In 1999 the founders of Google wanted to sell their company to one of its biggest competitors "Excite" for one million dollars but were rejected.

Fact 693: In order to prevent drunk driving, the Indian government passed a law stipulating that alcohol may only be sold at a distance of at least 1,640 feet from motorways. As a result, bars located near motorways built a "labyrinth" of walls to artificially extend the required distance from the motorway to the bar. To this day, the Indian government continues to allow these bars to serve alcohol.

Fact 694: During the Great Depression of the 1920s and 1930s, banker Pat Munroe advised his customers in the city of Quincy, Florida, to buy shares in the beverage company Coca-Cola. Over the next few years, the share price rose so much that countless people in Quincy quickly became millionaires and the city became the richest city in the USA.

Fact 695: If you twist both index fingers very slowly in a clockwise motion and then move them faster, the circles suddenly move in the opposite direction.

Fact 696: The actor Robin Williams was passionate about video games, which is the reason why he named his daughter "Zelda".

Fact 697: Geo-engineering refers to the use of technical means to influence chemical processes on Earth. In order to limit global warming, one of the topics discussed in this field of research is the introduction of reflecting particles into the atmosphere to partially reflect incoming solar rays.

Fact 698: There is a type of fungus that grows on ants and controls their behavior. The ant then has no control over its own body.

Fact 699: Because Donald Duck doesn't wear pants, his comics were banned in Finland for a long time.

Fact 700: On the basis of number of viewers, Disney's Jungle Book was the most successful movie in Germany.

Fact 701: Only three years after the first football rules were laid down, the hand play was forbidden.

Fact 702: The highest ever documented weight of a human being was 1,400 pounds.

Fact 703: The longest limousine in the world is almost 102 feet long and has 26 wheels. It is equipped with a king-size waterbed, a small helicopter landing pad and a swimming pool.

Fact 704: Jackie Chan's real name is "Chan Kong-Sang". He got the nickname "Jackie" during his time working construction. There, his colleagues were unable to pronounce his real name correctly and therefore called him "Little Jack" - after his boss Jack, who always took care of him. Over time, the name "Jackie" developed.

Fact 705: When the game "Twister" was released in 1966, it was described as "sex in a box".

Fact 706: The "dingo fence" is a fence in Australia designed to protect sheep in the southeast of the continent from predators. It has a total length of 3,363 miles.

Fact 707: With more than 100 million records sold, the Scorpions are the most successful German band.

Fact 708: In China, the websites of BBC News, Amnesty International and the Dalai Lama are banned for the citizens.

Fact 709: In ancient Babylon it was tradition for every woman to go to the Temple of Aphrodite at least once in her life to have sex with a stranger.

Fact 710: The astronomer Eugene Shoemaker is the only human whose ash was transported to the moon after his death.

Fact 711: The term "bug" for a programing error dates back to the 19th century. At the time, engineers were afraid that small bugs could destroy transmissions and cause malfunctions. When the computer was later invented, there were indeed several incidents in which insects caused a system to crash. With that, the term "bug" stuck once and for all.

Fact 712: The human eye already reached its final size at the age of three and no longer grows afterwards.

Fact 713: The deepest gold mine in the world is located in South Africa, and is situated 2.5 miles below the surface.

Fact 714: On the island of Yap in the western Pacific, the islanders used stone wheels as a monetary unit for centuries. The largest stone wheel had a diameter of 12 feet and weighed more than five tons.

Fact 715: In 1986, a Russian pilot bet his co-pilot that he could land an airplane without sight, using only the onboard instruments. To prove this, the two of them completely covered the windows of the plane and because of this negligence, the plane crashed. Of the 94 passengers, 70 died, but the pilot himself survived the accident.

Fact 716: Timothy Ray Brown is the first man to be cured from AIDS. In 2007 he received a bone marrow transplant due to his blood cancer. After the treatment, doctors could not detect HIV in his body anymore. To date, nobody knows how this was possible and whether the disease will come back. This phenomena could only be detected on two further people.

Fact 717: In summer the Eiffel Tower is 5.9 inches higher than in winter.

Fact 718: The Caspian Sea is the largest lake on earth. The largest freshwater lake in the world on the other hand is Lake Superior between Canada and the United States.

Fact 719: After Uber was introduced in New York City, the number of alcohol-related car accidents quickly dropped by more than 30 percent.

Fact 720: The 1996 Nokia Communicator was the first ever smartphone, it cost 800 dollars and even had a fax connection.

Fact 721: In Iceland, two-thirds of all university graduates are female.

Fact 722: Due to the decline of the lion population, there are now more lion statues worldwide than real lions.

Fact 723: A nap improves your memory and protects against heart disease.

Fact 724: Before the actor James Franco became successful, he practiced different accents while working as a cashier at McDonald's to see his customers reactions.

Fact 725: The Golden Gate Bridge has to be painted regularly. The salt water corrodes the paint so fast, that one has to start repainting the bridge as soon as one is finished painting it.

Fact 726: Based on an interview, Pope Francis watched television for the last time on the 15 July 1990.

Fact 727: In medieval castles, spiral staircases were always built clockwise, as this provided a tactical advantage. This made it harder for attackers to swing their swords without being hindered by the wall.

Fact 728: In 2008, a Brazilian tied 1,000 balloons to a chair and flew into the air. Two weeks later his corpse was found in the sea.

Fact 729: Although Beethoven has a song called "Fuer Elise", historians have proven that he did not know an Elise.

Fact 730: It is possible to tell from the dripping sound that a drop of water makes whether the water is warm or cold.

Fact 731: African-American Madam C. J. Walker, born in 1867 as Sarah Breedlove, developed a hair care product for black women that sold extremely well, making her the first female millionaire in the United States.

Fact 732: If the US state of California were a separate country, it would be the fifth largest economy in the world and thus economically larger than France or Great Britain.

Fact 733: Researchers believe that only ten percent of our seas are explored. This means we know less about our oceans than about the moon.

Fact 734: Africa is the world's second largest continent. Only Asia is larger.

Fact 735: Studies have proved that an increase in the amount of homework correlates with the increased likelihood of students to become depressed.

Fact 736: On 12 January 2007, the Washington Post launched an experiment with star violinist Joshua Bell. The musician dressed in street clothes and took his Stradivarius violin to an underground station in Washington, D.C., where he played pieces by Johann Sebastian Bach, Wolfgang Amadeus Mozart and Franz Schubert for over 40 minutes. Out of a total of 1,097 people who passed him, only seven stopped and he collected a total of 32.17 dollars. The average price for a seat at one of the artist's concerts is usually around 100 dollars.

Fact 737: Similar to the fingerprint, each human has an individual tongue print.

Fact 738: By licking a postage stamp, you consume 0,1 calories.

Fact 739: Before coffee became popular, beer was served for breakfast in the USA.

Fact 740: The sound that Pac-Man makes when he eats the little dots corresponds to the sound that comes from sticking your finger in your ear and moving it back and forth.

Fact 741: Hippos can sleep under water. A congenital reflex lets them drift to the surface while asleep in order to breathe and then to submerge again without waking up.

Fact 742: "Semantic saturation" describes the psychological phenomenon that a word temporarily seems to lose or change its meaning if you say or write it down too many times in a row.

Fact 743: The human is the only mammal which cannot swallow and breathe at the same time. We lose this ability when we start talking.

Fact 744: A type of jellyfish called the "sea wasp" is the most poisonous animal in the world.

Fact 745: Tupperware is named after its inventor, Earl Tupper.

Fact 746: Asian scalp hair grows about 20 percent faster than European scalp hair, while African scalp hair grows about 20 percent slower.

Fact 747: The likelihood of dying in your cab on the way to the airport is higher than to die on your flight.

Fact 748: The "Deep Lake" in Antarctica is so salty that even at a temperature of -20°C it does not freeze.

Fact 749: During the 18th century, the most important first aid measure for drowned people was to blow tobacco smoke into their rectum.

Fact 750: Sean Connery almost signed a contract with Manchester United.

Fact 751: The Kalasha are an indigenous people living in Pakistan. They consider themselves descendants of the ancient Greeks.

Fact 752: Penguins can jump six feet high.

Fact 753: The reason why actor Morgan Freeman wears earrings is due to a maritime tradition. They wore their earrings, so that their own burial could be paid with them, in case of their death.

Fact 754: Onoda Hirō was a Japanese intelligence officer who believed that the proclamation of the end of World War II was only a ruse by the Allies and therefore continued to hold his position 29 years after the end of the war. Only when his former superior, who was now a bookseller, visited him in 1974 could Onoda be convinced that the war was over.

Fact 755: Although women's brains are slightly smaller, they are more efficient than men's brains.

Fact 756: Every year, Finland grows by about 2.7 square miles. Due to melting glaciers, the land mass becomes lighter and slowly rises out of the sea.

Fact 757: E.T. was originally a horror movie, in which aliens reach the earth and kill humans by touching their heads with their fingers.

Fact 758: The clitoris has more than 8,000 nerve endings, while the penis just has 4,000.

Fact 759: NASA has special wristwatches produced for some of its employees that show the time of day on Mars.

Fact 760: The first deodorant for men was launched in 1935, although fragrance sprays for women had been around for decades. At the beginning of the 20th century, however, a strong smell in men was still considered masculine, so there was no demand for men's deodorants.

Fact 761: It is impossible to pinch your nose and say "Mhhh" for more than three seconds.

Fact 762: Queen Elizabeth uses her handbag to send secret signals to her employees. Changing the bag from one hand to the other, for example, constitutes a request to end the current conversation.

Fact 763: The embryos of the Sandtiger shark fight each other in the mother's womb. The surviving embryo will ultimately be born.

Fact 764: The bone density of people with a mutated LRP5 gene is eight times higher than in normal people. For these people, it is virtually impossible to suffer a fracture in a normal way.

Fact 765: All scenes of the children of Ted Mosby in "How I Met Your Mother" were shot during the first season.

Fact 766: With one pencil, one is able to draw a line with a length of up to 37 miles.

Fact 767: Until the 1960s, pregnancy tests were carried out by injecting a frog with the test person's urine. If the frog spawned within 12 to 24 hours, it could be assumed that the test person was pregnant.

Fact 768: Did you know that the the brain hides superfluous information, like the second "the" in this sentence?

Fact 769: In order to protect its population from a plague epidemic, the government of the Republic of Ragusa (now Croatia) decided in 1377 that arriving travelers and merchants had to go to a special hospital for 40 days before entering the city, in order to check whether they were carrying the pathogen. To this day, these 40 days (Latin: "quaranta") are regarded as the origin of the word "quarantine".

Fact 770: Fire does not cast a shadow.

Fact 771: In 2017, Ed Sheeran paid more taxes in the UK than Amazon and Starbucks.

Fact 772: Although woman are permitted to become pilots in Saudi Arabia it is prohibited for them to drive a car.

Fact 773: Listening to music is the only activity which involves all areas of the brain.

Fact 774: Assuming that Santa Claus has 34 hours to deliver all his gifts and only visits 800 million households around the world, his sled would have to be traveling at 99.99 percent of the speed of light.

Fact 775: In France people were killed by the guillotine up until 1977.

Fact 776: Asia has a larger surface area than the moon. While the surface of the moon measures only 14,645,698 square miles, Asia covers a total of 17,212,368 square miles.

Fact 777: Pierce Brosnan was contractually prohibited from wearing suits in other films during his time as James Bond.

Fact 778: After Tupac's death, his best friends mixed his ashes with marijuana and smoked it.

Fact 779: Hummingbirds use falcons as bodyguards. They frequently build their own nest directly underneath a falcon's nest, since falcons always look down on their prey from above and other animals therefore tend to avoid this area. Hummingbirds, on the other hand, are not hunted by falcons.

Fact 780: The likelihood of getting bitten by a human in New York is higher than the likelihood of getting bitten by a shark in the sea.

Fact 781: Neither Hollywood nor Bollywood produced the most movies per year. It is Nollywood in Nigeria, where about 2,000 movies are finished a year.

Fact 782: Sperm contains only five calories. So it only gets you fat when you are pregnant.

Fact 783: Women blink more frequently than men.

Fact 784: Leonid Rogozovy is the only human to do an appendectomy with local anaesthesia on himself.

Fact 785: The most common zodiac sign among billionaires is Aquarius. The least common one is Cancer.

Fact 786: Anthony Hopkins won an Oscar for Best Actor for his portrayal of Hannibal Lector in The Silence of the Lambs, although he only appeared in the movie for less than 17 minutes.

Fact 787: The shortest war in the world took place in 1896 between Zanzibar and the British. Zanzibar capitulated after only 38 minutes.

Fact 788: March 14th is the day of the number Pi. In the English notation 3/14, the date corresponds to the first three digits of the number.

Fact 789: The word Jedi from Star Wars comes from the Japanese word "Jidai-geki", which is a Japanese term for samurai movies.

Fact 790: George Washington was known to spend approximately seven percent of his annual salary on alcohol.

Fact 791: The medicine Imatinib is used to treat leukemia and costs 65,000 dollars for a year's supply. In India the same medicine is available for 2,500 dollars a year, because the pharma company could not patent it there.

Fact 792: Monopoly was developed in 1930 in the U.S. to create a pastime for the unemployed people during the great depression.

Fact 793: Taking into account the French overseas regions in the Pacific, Atlantic and Indian Oceans, France is the country with the most time zones. In total, there are twelve different ones.

Fact 794: The Indricotherium was the largest land mammal of all times and had no enemies to fear. The species could grow to almost 30 feet and weighed up to 22 tons. This made the giants almost ten feet taller than a giraffe and more than three times as heavy as an elephant.

Fact 795: There is a Barbie doll which is modelled after Angela Merkel.

Fact 796: At Christmas, the number of hits on divorce websites doubles.

Fact 797: In Night of the Living Dead (1968) zombies moved at one step per second. In World War Z (out today), they have sped up to 6.7 steps per second.

Fact 798: In China there is an app where you can order a "gangster", who can take care of your "enemies".

Fact 799: Octopus-Wrestling was a popular trend in the sixties. A diver grapples with an octopus in shallow water and tries to bring it to the surface.

Fact 800: During World War II, the Allies estimated the production rate of German tanks by comparing the serial numbers on captured tanks. The production rate of tanks was estimated at 256 units per month. After the end of the war, the actual production rate was discovered: 255 tanks per month.

Fact 801: The large yellow "M" in the McDonald's logo does not actually represent an "M", but rather the two original characteristic arches of McDonald's restaurants.

Fact 802: The Candlefish is so oily, that it used to be burned and used as a candle.

Fact 803: The names of the main characters in the film "Inception" are Dom, Robert, Eames, Arthur, Mal and Saito. When you combine the initial letters of these names, you get the word "Dreams".

Fact 804: The children of the nephews of Adolf Hitler had voluntarily sterilized themselves, in order for the Hitler bloodline to become extinct.

Fact 805: When Arnold Schwarzenegger wrote a veto letter to the State Assembly of California during his time as Governor of California, it turned out that the first letters of each line formed the word "Fuck You". At first, Schwarzenegger claimed that this was just a coincidence, but in his biography he later confirmed that he had intentionally placed this hidden message.

Fact 806: In Ethiopia, New Year's Eve is celebrated on 11 September, the calendar has 13 months and the year is counted seven years behind ours.

Fact 807: As part of a prank "hacker" attack, the activist group Anonymous sent a huge number of purely black faxes to Scientology to empty their printer cartridges.

Fact 808: When the first railroads started to operate, doctors warned of health effects, such as in the brain. This was due to its high speeds of up to 19 miles per hour.

Fact 809: Bill Clinton's real name is William Jefferson Clinton.

Fact 810: The brain takes about 0.6 seconds to choose the right word for a term.

Fact 811: Pizza Hut was the first pizza service to deliver a pizza to the International Space Station. In 2001, the company paid one million dollars to the Russian Space Agency for this promotional campaign.

Fact 812: When it was founded in 1953, Burger King was still called Insta-Burger King.

Fact 813: O. J. Simpson was freed, among other things, because it was proved that the investigator was biased. In a telephone conversation, he mentioned the word "Nigger" more than 40 times.

Fact 814: Muhammad Ali is the only famous person whose star on the "Walk of Fame" is not on the sidewalk itself but on the wall of a building. He did not want people trampling on his name.

Fact 815: If. There. Is. A. Period. After. Every. Word. Our. Brain. Automatically. Starts. Making. Pauses. After. Each. Word.

Fact 816: The vagina has a self-cleaning mechanism.

Fact 817: Of the 195 countries in the world, there are only 22 countries that have never been attacked or occupied by Britain.

Fact 818: Costa Rica does not have its own military anymore. Instead, the money is now spent on education and culture.

Fact 819: In 1755, Lisbon was hit by a strong earthquake that destroyed almost all the Catholic churches in the city, while all the city's brothels remained largely intact. The event ushered in a long-lasting crisis of faith in Portugal.

Fact 820: In 1983, 90 percent of US media were still in the hands of 50 different companies. Today, only six companies control 90 percent of the media landscape in the USA.

Fact 821: When McDonald's opened a restaurant in Rome in 1986, demonstrators handed out free pasta to counter McDonald's fast food.

Fact 822: During the Cold War, the Soviet Union launched the "Intervision Song Contest", the Soviet equivalent of the Eurovision Song Contest. However, since not every viewer had a telephone to vote on, the audience instead had to turn on the lights in their houses, if they liked the song, and turn them off, if they didn't. The local power station then used the electricity consumption to determine how many people had voted for a song.

Fact 823: There are the same amount of chickens and humans on Earth.

Fact 824: The US aircraft carrier USS Abraham Lincoln is operated by nuclear power and therefore only needs to be "refueled" every 25 years.

Fact 825: There are an estimated 500 million dogs on our planet.

Fact 826: Being in love releases the same hormones that the use of cocaine releases.

Fact 827: "May I have a large container of coffee". If you count the number of letters of every word in this sentence you get a good approximation for pi.

Fact 828: In the time since Pluto was discovered approximately 75 years ago, it has only traveled one third of its way around the sun.

Fact 829: In 2012, a new ant species was discovered in New York City. Scientists named it "ManhattAnt".

Fact 830: In 2009, Burger King launched a campaign where you could get a free burger if you unfriended ten friends on Facebook. The affected people then received a message that their friendship was worth less than a whopper. For image reasons, the campaign ended fairly quickly.

Fact 831: In 2010, General Electrics made profits of 14 billion dollars and paid not a penny in taxes.

Fact 832: Reading reduces your stress level much more than listening to music or walking.

Fact 833: One study has shown that black humor can indicate a particularly high IQ.

Fact 834: The Twitter account @everyword has tweeted every single word of the English language.

Fact 835: NASA has developed a device called "Finder" that can detect a person's breathing and heartbeat even under a 16-feet-thick layer of concrete. It was used to find buried people after the 2015 earthquake in Nepal.

Fact 836: In 1981 a hard disk containing one gigabyte cost 300,000 dollars.

Fact 837: A study came to the conclusion that the lack of exercise in the Western world kills the same amount of people as smoking does.

Fact 838: 66 million years ago, an asteroid with a diameter of 6.2 to 9.3 miles hit the Yucatan peninsula - at the time still a shallow sea. The Chicxulub impact had a force of at least 200 million Hiroshima bombs and directly and indirectly caused the extinction of up to 75 percent of all plant and animal species living at that time.

Fact 839: A positive pregnancy test in men may indicate testicular cancer.

Fact 840: About 75 percent of all people are scared of speaking publically in front of people.

Fact 841: In 2008, a female shark gave birth to a pup without having been previously fertilized. So far there are only two cases of asexual reproduction of sharks worldwide.

Fact 842: The English term "ultracrepidarianism" describes a person who tends to always express an opinion on a subject, even though he or she knows nothing about the topic.

Fact 843: Scientist Nikola Tesla had a strange peculiarity. He wanted all the number he encountered in everyday life to be divisible by three. For example, he would only move into a hotel room if its room number was a multiple of three.

Fact 844: Chris Putnam is a developer at Facebook and has immortalized himself in social networks. If one writes :putnam: in a comment, one will see his face as a smiley.

Fact 845: When cows eat too many carrots, their milk can turn pink.

Fact 846: The Cookie Monster from Sesame street is actually named "Sid"

Fact 847: The US secret service CIA bought the film rights to the books "Animal Farm" and "1984" from George Orwell in order to be able to use the films for their anti-communist propaganda.

Fact 848: Cobie Smulder, the Robin actor in "How I Met Your Mother", is actually Canadian.

Fact 849: The smell of rain on dry earth is called "petrichor".

Fact 850: The "Sacred Band of Thebes" was a special unit of the Theban army consisting exclusively of homosexual male couples. It was hoped that the soldiers would prove to be more cohesive, as they would try anything to save their partners.

Fact 851: In ancient Greece the sandals of prostitutes bared an inscription, so that the words "follow me" appeared on the sandy ground.

Fact 852: The average depth of our oceans is 12,467 feet. The deepest point, the Mariana Trench, is even approximately 36,201 feet below sea level.

Fact 853: Female lions carry out 90 percent of the lion's hunting activities.

Fact 854: The founder of Wikipedia - Jimmy Wales - has only a fortune of about one million dollars.

Fact 855: After saffron, vanilla is the second most expensive spice in the world. In 2017, one kilo of black vanilla pods cost up to 600 dollars. Saffron of average quality costs up to 5,000 dollars.

Fact 856: A study from 2002 showed that 60 percent of people cannot have a ten minute conversation without having lied at least once.

Fact 857: About 90 percent of people won't find the the mistake   in   here: A,B,C,D,E,F,G,H,I,J,K,L,M,N,O,P,Q,R,S,T,U,V,W,X,Y,Z.

Fact 858: Sleeping on your belly can lead to crazier, creepier and more sexual dreams.

Fact 859: In 1862, former slave Robert Smalls stole a Confederate ship and handed it over to the Union army. He was given command of the ship, promoted to Major General after several years and ultimately bought the house in which he had been held as a slave. He taught himself to read and write, ran for Congress, and was elected five times in a row.

Fact 860: Almost all windmills in the world rotate counterclockwise, while almost all wind turbines in the world rotate clockwise.

Fact 861: Pirates wore an eye patch, so they could take it off at night and so could see better in the dark.

Fact 862: Archer Matt Stutzman holds the world record for the longest shot with a bow and arrow under Olympic conditions. He hit his mark at a distance of 930 feet. What makes this so special is the fact that due to a disability, Matt Stutzman has no arms and therefore uses the bow with his feet.

Fact 863: The release of the film "The Princess and the Frog" led to more than 50 cases in the US where children were infected with a disease because they had kissed a frog.

Fact 864: In one second an average of two people die.

Fact 865: Whales can reach a volume of up to 230 decibels with their songs. That is twice as loud as a jet taking off.

Fact 866: The anchor motif as a tattoo was originally meant to signal that the carrier had already crossed the Atlantic.

Fact 867: In terms of GDP growth, Ethiopia was the fastest growing economy in the world in 2017.

Fact 868: Dogs are red-green blind.

Fact 869: After watching the series "Breaking Bad", Hannibal actor Anthony Hopkins wrote a letter to Bryan Cranston, the main character of the series, and told him: "Your performance as Walter White was the best acting I have seen - ever".

Fact 870: Africa consists of 54 countries and with the Western Sahara also a non-self-governing territory.

Fact 871: The U.S. Navy now uses Xbox 360 controllers to control its periscopes. The soldiers find the controller much easier to use, while at the same time the costs of the control units have declined drastically.

Fact 872: The classic film "One flew over the cuckoo's nest" with Jack Nicholson was actually shot in a mental hospital. Many of the patients featured in the movie were actually being treated there at the time.

Fact 873: The website www.poopsenders.com allows you to order the faeces of different types of animals and have them sent them to somebody else.

Fact 874: The abbreviation "SOS" actually has no real meaning and was originally introduced only because of the special Morse coding of the three letters (...---...). The widely-known interpretation "Save our Souls" was only developed later on.

Fact 875: The word "blood" is mentioned at least once in every Shakespeare piece.

Fact 876: If you Google "241543903" you get numerous pictures of people who have put their heads in the refrigerator.

Fact 877: Drug baron Pablo Escobar offered Colombia to pay off the country's entire foreign debt of 20 billion dollars if it did not extradite him to the USA.

Fact 878: To date, about 5,000 people have already turned their ashes into an artificial diamond after death.

Fact 879: Regardless of body size, all mammals take an average of about 21 seconds to empty their bladders. Scientists refer to this as the "law of urination".

Fact 880: In ancient Rome the punishment for rapists was their genitals being smashed between two stones.

Fact 881: In the history of Mexico, on one occasion, there were three presidents on one day.

Fact 882: Scorpions can survive up to two years without food.

Fact 883: Octopi have three hearts.

Fact 884: Most board games are sold in Germany.

Fact 885: The real Top Gun School imposes a five dollar fine to anyone in the staff that quotes the movie.

Fact 886: 90 percent of all people live in the northern hemisphere.

Fact 887: In Finland, Valentine's Day is called Ystävänpäivä ("Friends' Day"). So there, the day is not only dedicated to one's partner, but also to one's circle of friends.

Fact 888: Africa is the only continent that's surface extends from a northern temperate zone to a southern temperate zone.

Fact 889: The shoe size of the Statue of Liberty is size 879.

Fact 890: American Express credit card numbers always start with a three, Visa cards with a four, Mastercards with a five and Discover Cards with a six.

Fact 891: Thanks to collaboration with Twitter, every public tweet sent in the U.S., is digitally archived in the Library of Congress.

Fact 892: If you visit a Jewish grave, it is common practice to leave a small stone as a symbol of mourning and remembrance. The tradition dates back to a time when all Jewish graves were still in the desert. In order to prevent scavengers from digging up the corpses, the mourners erected pyramids of small stones.

Fact 893: A koala's fingerprint is so similar to that of a human being that there have been several cases in Australia with considerable confusion about the perpetrator at a crime scene.

Fact 894: If you were to stack all the viruses in the world on top of each other, this would result in a tower that would extend far beyond the moon, even further than our sun, further than Alpha Centauri and further than the edge of the Milky Way and into the next galaxy, with a total height of about 200 million light years.

Fact 895: In the U.S. most movies are released on Independence Day. Conversely, the movie "Independence Day" was released a week prior to Independence Day.

Fact 896: In 1893, a U.S. citizen made an application to change the name of the country to "The United States of the Earth".

Fact 897: Months beginning with a Sunday always have a Friday 13th.

Fact 898: In Singapore, it is forbidden to chew gum. Only a few people are allowed to do so for medical reasons.

Fact 899: Reinhold Messner climbed Nanga Parbat, the ninth highest mountain in the world, a total of three times. The first time, his brother died on the way up and he himself lost seven toes. He decided to climb the mountain again and was the first person to do so on his own. On his third ascent, he finally climbed the mountain in memory of his deceased brother, so that both brothers ended up climbing the mountain together - at least symbolically.

Fact 900: Butterflies are cannibals.

Fact 901: The inventor of cotton candy was also a practicing dentist.

Fact 902: The Harvard physicist Lene Hau was successful in reducing the speed of light to 38 miles per hour.

Fact 903: For years, Liechtenstein and Haiti had the same flag, which was only noticed when the two nations met at the 1936 Olympic Games. A year later, the flag of Liechtenstein was therefore adorned with the symbol of a golden princely hat.

Fact 904: In preparation for his role as Walter White in "Breaking Bad" Bryan Cranston was taught by the DEA how to make meth.

Fact 905: A study proved that 70 percent of women prefer to eat chocolate rather than have sex.

Fact 906: The song "Hey ya" by Outkast says "Shake it like a Polaroid picture", forced Polaroid to release a press release that shaking a Polaroid too much can damage the picture.

Fact 907: Nintendo's "Mario" character is named after Mario Segale. He was the landlord of the first warehouse where Nintendo worked.

Fact 908: The average age of soldiers fighting in Vietnam was 19. During World War II it was 26.

Fact 909: In addition to the known blood types of the AB0 system, there is a fourth, very rare variant. It is colloquially called the Bombay blood group, since only about 20,000 people worldwide have this blood group, almost all of whom come from India.

Fact 910: A blowjob under water is called "Aquabob".

Fact 911: The maiden name of Goethe's mother was "Textor".

Fact 912: Australia exports camels to Saudi Arabia.

Fact 913: Washing your hands regularly with soap and water is a sufficiently protective mechanism against the Ebola virus.

Fact 914: Bulletproof glass can be made in such a way that it is bulletproof only from one side and allows bullets to pass through from the other.

Fact 915: The first Subway restaurant was opened in 1965 by a 17-year-old high school graduate looking for a way to finance his tuition fees.

Fact 916: Over 50% of the African population is under the age of 25.

Fact 917: The heart of a shrimp is located in its head.

Fact 918: Only two percent of all people have green eyes.

Fact 919: It is impossible to cause your own death by strangling yourself.

Fact 920: During the hostage situation at the Dubrovka Theatre in Moscow in 2002, special units used the narcotic carfentanyl, which is otherwise only used to stun big game like elephants, in their attempt to free the hostages. Due to insufficient medical care after the chemical attack, 125 hostages died as a result of the use of gas, but only five by the hands of the hostage-takers.

Fact 921: During the 19th century in the UK, the sentence for an unsuccessful suicide attempt was death by hanging.

Fact 922: "Paruresis" is the fear that makes it impossible for people to urinate when other people are around.

Fact 923: The world's first vibrator was patented in 1869 and was powered by a small steam engine.

Fact 924: Valentina Tereshkova, sent into space in 1963, was the first woman in space. To this day, she remains the only woman to have been on a space mission alone. She was alone in space for a total of three days and orbited the Earth a total of 48 times.

Fact 925: There are no family names in Ethiopia. Instead, a child's surname is simply their father's first name.

Fact 926: Four out of five people sing in the car.

Fact 927: With almost 280,000 visitors, the Frankfurt Book Fair is the largest book fair in the world.

Fact 928: In 1835, an assassin tried to kill the King of France Louis Philippe I with a homemade rifle. Due to the rifle's poor construction, however, it exploded before the assassination attempt, killing 18 passers-by. The King of France himself was only slightly wounded.

Fact 929: When King Conrad III took Weinsberg Castle in 1140, he promised all the women in the castle free passage and allowed them to take with them all the belongings they could carry on their backs. So the women decided to carry their husbands out of the castle on their backs, thereby saving their lives. To this day, the ruins of the castle still bear the nickname "Weibertreu" (faithful women).

Fact 930: The highest waterfall in the world is Salto Ángel in Venezuela with a height of 3,212 feet.

Fact 931: The slogan of Vermin Supreme, a candidate for the U.S. presidency, was "Free ponies for all Americans".

Fact 932: Before "James Bond" actor Daniel Craig became a professional actor, he could not afford to pay his rent. Because of this he often slept on park benches.

Fact 933: Sleep researchers have confirmed that women need more sleep than men and are more likely to suffer health damage if they do not get enough sleep.

Fact 934: Cherophobia is the fear of fun.

Fact 935: Only a few special types of piranhas eat meat. All others feed on plants.

Fact 936: To date, 43 Germans have won an Oscar and 81 have been awarded the Nobel Prize.

Fact 937: Some survivors of Hiroshima showed an unusual reaction. Due to the high radiation dose they were subjected to, their finger nails turned black and bled slightly when cut.

Fact 938: During World War II, Queen Elizabeth worked as a mechanic for the British troops.

Fact 939: A Scottish study found that most heart attacks happen on a Monday.

Fact 940: It is now assumed that the United States carried out a total of 638 assassination attempts on Fidel Castro. Among other things, these included poisoned cigars, contaminated diving equipment, an exploding cigar and a poisoned ballpoint pen.

Fact 941: The US presidential limousine "The Beast" even contains blood reserves in the president's blood type.

Fact 942: Cress can be sown on paper and harvested after only four days.

Fact 943: The most common cause of death in Germany for men and women is coronary heart disease.

Fact 944: The first president of Zimbabwe was President Canaan Banana.

Fact 945: The Russian Fyodor Vasilyev holds the record for most children fathered by a man with a woman. In the 18th century, his wife gave birth to a total of 69 children, including four sets of quadruplets, seven sets of triplets and 16 pairs of twins. Later on, he married again and fathered another 18 children with his second wife, including two sets of triplets and six pairs of twins.

Fact 946: The Chupa Chups logo was designed by Salvador Dali.

Fact 947: "The Pineapple Incident" is the most watched episode of "How I Met Your Mother".

Fact 948: Africa is only the world's second driest continent. Australia is drier.

Fact 949: In the US state of Illinois, there is a restaurant called "Burger King" that is not part of the fast food chain. Since the restaurant secured the rights to the name earlier, it won the legal dispute with the Burger King chain. To this day, the franchise is not allowed to open a branch within a radius of 20 miles.

Fact 950: When in England the packaging of the drug Tylenol was changed from a bottle to a blister pack, the suicide rate involving the drug decreased by more than 50 percent. Instead of taking several tablets out of the container at once, each tablet had to be squeezed out of the blister pack individually, giving people more time to reconsider their suicide attempt.

Fact 951: When the Cornhuskers - the football team of the University of Nebraska- have a home match, the stadium becomes the third biggest city in the state.

Fact 952: In Iowa, a 99 year old senior woman sews one dress every day to donate them to children in Africa.

Fact 953: The Arabic number system used around the globe today was originally developed in India and was only disseminated throughout the world by Arabic researchers.

Fact 954: If a teacher punishes an entire school class for an individual student's misconduct, this is an unlawful collective punishment and is classified as a war crime under Article 87(3) of the Third Geneva Convention and Article 33 of the Fourth Geneva Convention.

Fact 955: In Turkmenistan, water, gas and electricity has been free to citizens since 1991.

Fact 956: In Alaska there is a sand desert with dunes up to 160 feet high.

Fact 957: In 1994 the iPad would have been the fastest computer on earth.

Fact 958: Based on current extrapolations Bill Gates could be the first trillionaire in the world.

Fact 959: Nuclear divers are professional divers who carry out repair and cleaning work in the water of the cooling systems of nuclear reactors.

Fact 960: The "Lady Macbeth effect" is the phenomenon of wanting to wash yourself physically, even if you have only "dirtied" yourself mentally. If a person is ashamed of an event, he or she will find it liberating to take a shower.

Fact 961: In the fun sport Headis, two players compete against each other following the rules of table tennis. However, the game is played with a special ball the size of a football, which may only be touched with the head. In 2017 the twelfth Headis World Championships were held.

Fact 962: The genetic defect "congenital analgesia" causes the affected person to feel absolutely to pain. In 2006, a 14-year-old suffering from this genetic defect jumped off a roof to show his friends that he does not feel pain. However, he died as a result of the injuries sustained during impact.

Fact 963: In the U.S. the most dangerous job is to be a fisherman. Approximately one out of every 900 die during work.

Fact 964: Thomas Stevens is considered to be the first person to have circumnavigated the world on a bicycle. From April 1884 to December 1886, he rode around the globe on a penny-farthing.

Fact 965: Your mouth contains more bacteria than your anus.

Fact 966: When the Big Bang theory was presented for the first time, it was rejected by many scientists because it seemed too religious.

Fact 967: "Broken Heart Syndrome" is the medical term for the separation of a beloved partner. The symptoms can be so strong, that the patient gets cardiac dysrhythmia, suffers from pain and is not able to breathe properly.

Fact 968: In May 2015, 2.3 million Americans were still logging on to the Internet using a 56k modem and an old AOL access.

Fact 969: In Japan, a woman was sentenced to death in 2017 for killing her three husbands with poison between 2007 and 2012. Previously, she had searched dating portals for wealthy men in order to marry them and then acquire their assets through violent death. She managed to make about 7.7 million euros with this strategy. She therefore became known as the "Black Widow".

Fact 970: The record for the longest time between the birth of twins is 87 days. One of the children was premature, while the other remained in the mother's womb until the regular birth.

Fact 971: Wombat excrements are cube-shaped. So far, we have not been able to determine the evolutionary advantage of excreta in this shape. It is assumed, however, that it allows the animals to better mark their territory.

Fact 972: In Brazil, a termite mound was discovered that is probably up to 4,000 years old - almost as old as the pyramids in Egypt.

Fact 973: The abbreviation "X-Mas" for Christmas can be traced back to the ancient Greeks. The X stands for the Greek letter "Chi" which used to be the abbreviation for the word Christ.

Fact 974: George Washington was known to convince voters with the help of alcohol. At an election campaign with over 400 people, he brought over 500 liters of alcohol to secure their votes.

Fact 975: It takes over 15 million Lego bricks to re-create everything from "The Lego Movie".

Fact 976: People with red hair are more resistant to anesthetics.

Fact 977: The vertical groove that runs from the nose to the center of the upper lip is called "philtrum".

Fact 978: The metal tip of a shoelace is called an aglet.

Fact 979: Octopuses have a favorite arm. They tend to use this arm more often, for example to grab prey.

Fact 980: Falling asleep next to a loved one helps one to doze off faster and decreases the risk of depression.

Fact 981: If you tell yourself that you slept well last night even though you didn't, you will still feel less tired. This is called placebo sleep.

Fact 982: Scientists of Stanford University observed that a walk can increase people's creativity by up to 60 percent.

Fact 983: Schwuugle describes itself as "the gay search engine".

Fact 984: A Rubik's Cube with three times three pieces offers 43,252,003,274,489,856,000 different combinations.

Fact 985: The Eiffel Tower was only built for the 1889 World Exhibition and was supposed to be demolished 20 years later.

Fact 986: Approximately eight percent of human DNA is from the DNA of viruses that infected humans thousands of years ago.

Fact 987: Reed Hasting, the founder of Netflix, came up with the idea for the streaming service after forgetting to return a rental DVD and paying $40 for it.

Fact 988: A liger is a cross between a lion and a tiger. They are the largest cats of prey in the world and can weigh up to 990 pounds.

Fact 989: During the 1904 Summer Olympics in St. Louis, the American Frederick Lorz was the first to reach the finish line of the marathon race. It turned out, however, that he had covered about half the distance by car.

Fact 990: In Denmark, there is a tradition that if you are not married by your 25th birthday, your friends and family will shower you with cinnamon.

Fact 991: The mad hatter from "Alice in Wonderland" is based on the fact that in the 18th century hatmakers often suffered from mental illnesses. For a long time, people were not sure why this was the case, but then they discovered that the mercury used by hatmakers to make hats caused mental disorders.

Fact 992: When Einstein heard of the book "100 Authors Against Albert Einstein," he replied, "Why 100? If I were wrong, one would be enough."

Fact 993: Ten percent of all car accidents are caused by being distracted, for example when writing an SMS.

Fact 994: During World War II, the Syrian brown bear "Wojtek" repeatedly supported Polish soldiers by bringing important military transports to them on the battlefield. In return, he was awarded the rank of non-commissioned officer.

Fact 995: Finland was the first country in the world to make broadband Internet access a legal right. If a house does not have a broadband connection, a Finish tenant can sue his or her landlord or the city.

Fact 996: Due to reduced air pressure, water on Mount Everest boils at 158 degrees Fahrenheit.

Fact 997: Today, the Earth is surrounded by so much space debris that in the near future it may even be dangerous to leave the Earth in a spaceship. This phenomenon is also known as the Kessler syndrome.

Fact 998: An average cloud weighs about 1.5 million pounds.

Fact 999: You can't commit suicide by holding your breath.

Fact 1000: Scientists assume that the face of the Sphinx was painted red.